D0856041

RIFAT SONSINO
DANIEL B. SYME

What Happens
After I Die?

Jewish Views of Life
After Death

JASON ARONSON INC.
Northvale, New Jersey
London

To the memory of my father-in-law
Dr. Israel Goldstein
Rifat Sonsino

For my parents, M. Robert and Sonia Syme
My wife, Deborah Shayne Syme
My son, Joshua Shayne Syme
My brothers, David Syme and Michael Syme ז״ל ,
who touched my life in this world,
whatever lies beyond
Daniel B. Syme

Copyright © 1994 by Jason Aronson Inc.
Copyright © 1990 by UAHC Press

10 9 8 7 6 5 4 3 2 1

Library of Congress Cataloging-in-Publication Data

Sonsino, Rifat, 1938-
    What happens after I die? : Jewish views of life after death /
Rifat Sonsino, Daniel B. Syme.—1st Jason Aronson Inc. ed.
        p. cm.
    Previously published: New York, N.Y. : UAHC Press, c1990.
    Includes bibliographical references.
    ISBN 1-56821-288-7
    1. Immortality—Judaism—History of doctrines. 2. Future life—
Judaism—History of doctrines. 3. Judaism—Doctrines. I. Syme,
Daniel B. II. Title.
[BM645.I5S66 1994]
296.3′3—dc20   94-13625

Manufactured in the United States of America. Jason Aronson Inc. offers books and cassettes. For information and catalog write to Jason Aronson Inc., 230 Livingston Street, Northvale, New Jersey.

Published to
honor the memory of
I.H. and Anna Grancell

Acknowledgments

This volume has benefited from the wisdom and counsel of many individuals. First and foremost, we are indebted to the Jewish leaders whose own introspective thinking is contained herein: Rabbis Alexander M. Schindler and Harold M. Schulweis, Doctors Eugene B. Borowitz and Alvin J. Reines, and Arlene Agus and Blu Greenberg.

We express our thanks to those rabbis, educators, and lay leaders who read the manuscript in various stages and offered many helpful comments: Rabbis Gary Bretton-Granatoor, Samuel Karff, Howard Laibson, Jack Stern, Jr., Sheldon Zimmerman, and Bernard Zlotowitz. We extend our gratitude also to Irving Konigsberg, Lydia Kukoff, Norma Levitt, Elaine Merians, Linda Merians, Joyce Ottenheimer, Margery Rothschild, Jocelyn Rudner, Norman Schwartz, Evely Laser Shlensky, B. J. Tanenbaum, Jr., and Paul Uhlmann, Jr.

As always, we express heartfelt appreciation to Aron Hirt-Manheimer, Stuart Benick, Annette Abramson, and Dorian Kreindler of the UAHC Department of Publications. They took the raw manuscript and transformed it into a living book with their special and creative magic.

And finally we express our deep gratitude to Eppie Begleiter, Muriel Freedman, and Vivian Mendeles, who typed this manuscript time and time again, who urged us on, and who gave us strength.

Rifat Sonsino
Daniel B. Syme

"If a man dies, can he live again?"
Job 14:14

"I don't want to attain immortality through my work.
I want to attain immortality by not dying."
Woody Allen

Contents

Introduction   ix

Abbreviations   xi

Part One—Classic Jewish Positions

1 · After Death, Perhaps Nothing   3

2 · Down to Sheol   10

3 · Resurrection of the Body and Soul, Hell and Paradise   21

4 · Immortality   36

5 · Reincarnation   46

6 · Living on through Deeds   55

Bibliography   62

Part Two—Contemporary Thinkers

7 · Here and Hereafter   69
   RABBI ALEXANDER M. SCHINDLER

8 · Is There Life After Death?   79
   BLU GREENBERG

9 · Immortality through Goodness and Activism   96
   RABBI HAROLD M. SCHULWEIS

viii ·   *Contents*

10 · Covenant Theology   107
  DR. EUGENE B. BOROWITZ

11 · Outrage and Faith   116
  ARLENE AGUS

12 · Death and Afterexistence: A Polydox View   126
  DR. ALVIN J. REINES

13 · Two Personal Statements   142
  RABBI DANIEL B. SYME

  RABBI RIFAT SONSINO

In Conclusion   146

Introduction

In our previous volume, *Finding God,* we introduced ten distinct ways in which great Jewish thinkers spoke and wrote about the search for the Divine. In the course of this book, we address a spectrum of Jewish responses to the question of life after death. Time and time again, we confront this, the most profound of all human existential dilemmas. Does Judaism have something to say about this matter, and if so, what?

Part One of this book presents six classical Jewish answers drawn from the Tanach (Hebrew Bible), rabbinic commentaries, medieval thinkers, mystical literature, and writers of the nineteenth and twentieth centuries.

In Part Two of the book, we confront the personal notions of life after death espoused by contemporary thinkers from virtually all streams of the Jewish community. Each of these well-known writers, educators, and Jewish leaders found the challenge compelling and often painful. Yet their words to us today are as important to the quest as any that have preceded them in the totality of Jewish experience; they are fellow Jews who are contemplating the mystery of the unknown.

Finally, we have appended our personal ideas at the conclusion of this second section. We believe we owe our readers a clear explanation of where we stand as well.

As with *Finding God,* we hope you will discover within these pages at least one thinker whose ideas resonate with your own. If so, you will have rooted yourself in the Jewish spiritual world and found a "friend" whose writings you may wish to peruse more intensively. At the very least, however, we trust that this book will open your mind to the richness of our Jewish heritage in this realm. We need not look elsewhere for answers to our quest.

Abbreviations

B.B.	Baba Batra	NJV	New Jewish Version
B.M.	Baba Metzia		(JPS Bible)
Ber.	Berachot	Num.	Numbers
Chron.	Chronicles	Prov.	Proverbs
Deut.	Deuteronomy	Pes.	Pesachim
Eccles.	Ecclesiastes	Ps.	Psalms
Ed.	Eduyot	R.H.	Rosh Hashanah
Exod.	Exodus	RSV	Revised Standard
Ezek.	Ezekiel		Version (Oxford
Gen.	Genesis		Annotated Bible—
Hag.	Chagigah		Old and New
Isa.	Isaiah		Testament)
Jer.	Jeremiah	Sam.	Samuel
Jon.	Jonah	San.	Sanhedrin
Ket.	Ketubot	Shab.	Shabbat
Kid.	Kiddushin	Ta'an.	Ta'anit
Lam.	Lamentations	Tos.	Tosefta
Lev.	Leviticus		

Authors' Note

Because the Hebrew Bible uses the masculine form, Bible translators and many writers refer to God as "He."

In the text of this book, except in direct quotations, we have remained true to our conviction, shared by many thinkers, that God is beyond gender, neither male nor female.

All biblical quotes are taken from *Tanach, A New Translation of the Holy Scriptures According to the Traditional Hebrew Text*. Philadelphia: Jewish Publication Society, 1985.

Part I
CLASSIC JEWISH POSITIONS

· 1 ·

After Death,
Perhaps Nothing

Death Is a Part of Life

Death transcends human comprehension. No one has ever had an "experience" of death. Even those who claim they have "died" and "come back" can, in truth, speak only of a "near-death experience." Because of the limitations of the human mind, a genuine understanding of death will inevitably elude even the wisest of us. As the Reform prayer book, *Gates of Prayer* (GOP), puts it: "What can we know of death, we who cannot understand life?"[1]

Judaism regards death as an inevitable part of life. Just as we are born, so we must die. "What man can live and not see death . . . ?" (Ps. 89:49, NJV). No one and nothing lives forever. Thus, we accept death, however grudgingly. The rabbis of old expressed this notion by affirming: "Those who are born are destined to die. . . . You were created against your will. . . . Despite your wishes you live, and against your will you shall die" (*Avot* 4:22).

In rabbinic thinking, life and death are usually seen as parallel processes.

> As a man enters [the world] so he departs. He enters it with a cry and departs from the world with a cry. . . . He enters the world with a sigh and takes leave of it with a sigh. . . . It has been taught in the name of Rabbi Meir: When a person enters the world his hands are clenched as though to say "The

3

whole world is mine, I shall inherit it"; but when he takes
leave of it his hands are spread open as though to say "I have
inherited nothing from the world."

(*Eccles. Rabbah* 5:14, Soncino)

Commenting on a verse in the creation story of the Bible—"It
was very good" (Gen. 1:31)—one of the rabbis interpreted the
phrase to mean that death is an integral part of the natural order,
which is "good" (*Gen. Rabbah* 9:5).

Intellectual acceptance of death, however, does not allay human
anxiety about our finitude. Intellectually we may realize that "if
there were no such thing as death, soon there would be no room
on this earth for further births."[2] Similarly, as the *Gates of Repentance*
expresses it:

> If some messenger were to come to us with the offer that
> death should be overthrown, but with the one inseparable condi-
> tion that birth should also cease; if the existing generation were
> given the chance to live forever, but on the clear understanding
> that never again would there be a child, or a youth, or first
> love, never again new persons with new hopes, new ideas, new
> achievements; ourselves for always and never any others—could
> the answer be in doubt?"[3]

But, emotionally, as the modern Orthodox rabbi Maurice Lamm
points out: "Death is the crisis of life. How a man handles death
indicates a great deal about how he approaches life. As there is a
Jewish way of life, there is a Jewish way of death."[4]

Judaism has responded to this deeply felt human need and
throughout the ages tried to create patterns of thought and action
to help us face the death of a loved one and prepare to go on
living.

Death Makes Life Precious

It is almost impossible for us to fathom living a purposeful life
"forever." In fact, the recognition that our days are numbered gives

us perspective. Rabbi Joshua L. Liebman wrote, "I often feel that death is not the enemy of life, but its friend, for it is the knowledge that our years are limited which makes them so precious."[5]

According to Rabbi Liebman, this precious quality of life is a major source of our creativity. In the words of *Gates of Prayer:* "Just because we are human, we are prisoners of the years. Yet that very prison is the room of discipline in which we, driven by the urgency of time, create" (p. 625).

Hope for Immortality

The pursuit of immortality has been a dominant theme of world literature.

In one of the oldest epics in the ancient Near Eastern literature, a powerful king named Gilgamesh learns the secret of how to defy death from Utnapishtim, the great hero of the Babylonian Deluge. However, when a serpent snuffs out the fragrance of the magical plant the king is about to eat, his dream of immortality is dashed, and he resigns himself to his fate as a mortal.

In a similar Babylonian story, Adapa, the caretaker of the city of Eridu, misses a chance to obtain immortality when the gods trick him. Though bitterly disappointed, Adapa becomes the wisest of people, thereby achieving a measure of consolation.

Early in the Hebrew Bible, the issue of immortality causes discord between God and the first humans. Having eaten from the tree of knowledge of good and bad, Adam readies himself to eat from the tree of life, and thus to live forever. At this point, God intervenes:

> And the Lord God said, "Now that the man has become like one of us, knowing good and bad, what if he should stretch out his hand and take also from the tree of life and eat, and live forever!" So the Lord God banished him from the Garden of Eden, to till the soil from which he was taken. He drove the man out, and stationed east of the Garden of Eden the cherubim and the fiery ever-turning sword, to guard the way to the tree of life. (Gen. 3:22–24)

Judaism has always taught that human beings are destined to die.

"Early or late," the *Gates of Prayer* tells us, "all must answer the summons to return to the Reservoir of Being" (p. 627). Life has a beginning as well as an end. Alvin Fine calls it "a sacred pilgrimage."

> Birth is a beginning,
> And death a destination;
> But life is a journey,
> A sacred pilgrimage
> Made stage by stage—
> From birth to death
> to life everlasting.[6]

Why Persist?

Why has humanity persisted in probing the mysteries of death? Perhaps for no other reason than simple curiosity. The unknown we face at life's end challenges our reason and imagination. Simple curiosity, however, may be an insufficient motive to explain this human concern. In *Wings of the Morning*, Rabbi Roland B. Gittelsohn lists five additional reasons:

1. Fear of death. We know the difference between sleeping and death. We are afraid that the latter will carry us off forever.
2. Our deep sorrow when people dear to us pass away. We yearn to know what happened to our deceased loved ones. We care for them in death, as we did in life.
3. Our deep love for life. This makes us wonder not only what happens in life but in death as well.
4. Our desire to remain creative. We seek to know whether or not death terminates our achievements.
5. Our conviction that righteousness must prevail over injustice, that the thrust of moral evolution will continue.[7]

These and similar concerns have propelled human beings to look beyond life on earth. Jewish thinkers, like those in other religions, have formed various viewpoints. None of them, however, represents "the" Jewish answer. Though life beyond the grave in some form was affirmed by rabbinic sages and Jewish philosophers, there has always been room for further exploration.

After Death—Nothing

There is no proof of life beyond the grave. Some Jewish thinkers, in fact, have suggested that the idea of the hereafter is psychologically motivated, a projection of a human need, a wish fulfillment. In an essay entitled "Past and Future," Asher Ginsberg (1856–1927), who wrote under the pen name Ahad Ha-Am, argued that the individual must die but not the nation:

> The individual dies: die he must; all his hopes for the future cannot save him from death. But the nation has a spiritual thread of life, and physical laws do not set a limit to its years or its strength. And so, let it but make the future an integral part of its self, though it be only in the form of a fanciful hope . . .[8]

In his essay "Flesh and Spirit," Ginsberg maintained that the desire for existence forces people "to seek consolation not only against the sufferings of the life that is theirs today but also against the bitterness of the death that tomorrow will bring. Not finding what they want in the real world, they arrive finally at the idea of a world beyond nature and transfer the center of gravity of their ego from the body to the soul."[9]

Sigmund Freud (1856–1939), the founder of psychoanalysis, took this idea a step further, arguing that religious dogma, including the belief in a future life, is simply an "illusion." "Wish-fulfillment," he writes, "is a prominent factor in its [religious dogma's] motivation, while disregarding its relations to reality . . ."[10]

Freud added that the whole idea of immortality is a sign of our despair and limitation, invented to compensate for the misery of our life on earth. In reality, death is annihilation, a return to "inorganic lifelessness." Religion, as "the universal obsessional neurosis of humanity,"[11] includes the belief in an afterlife as a way to satisfy the human need for overcoming the existential problems of the day. In reality, Freud claimed a self-asserting individual has no need for a childish expectation of a future life. In fact, he saw the idea of immortality as a way of retreating from the challenges of this world into a world of myth and fantasy.

The denial of life after death has a small number of proponents among religious thinkers as well. Among Jews, the most vocal is Rabbi Richard L. Rubenstein, who wrote in a personal statement on Judaism:

> Even as a child . . . I believed that when I died the whole world of my existence would disappear with me. My world would last only as long as I did. I was convinced that I had arisen out of nothingness and was destined to return to nothingness. All human beings were locked in the same fatality. In the final analysis, omnipotent nothingness was lord of all creation. Nothing in the bleak, cold, unfeeling universe was remotely concerned with human aspiration and longing. Even as a rabbi, I have never really departed from my earliest primordial feelings about my place in the cosmos.[12]

If we agree with Rubenstein, we should not even hope for immortality. Instead we should concern ourselves solely with the tasks of life. He writes:

> Only death perfects life and ends its problems. God can only redeem by slaying. We have nothing to hope for beyond what we are capable of creating in the time we have allotted to us. Of course, this leaves room for much to do and much to create. Nevertheless, in the final analysis all things crumble away into the nothingness which is at the beginning and end of creation.[13]

After Death—Who Knows?

Not all Jewish thinkers who entertain doubts about the hereafter deny its existence. Those who express skepticism yet are unwilling to deny the possibility of immortality are called "agnostics" (from the Greek, meaning "unknown"). They maintain that the human mind is incapable of knowing what lies beyond material phenomena and therefore refrain from accepting or rejecting its existence.

One of the great contemporary Orthodox Jewish thinkers who has maintained an agnostic position is British scholar Rabbi Louis Jacobs. In his words:

> Religious agnosticism in some aspects of this whole area is not only legitimate but altogether desirable. As Maimonides [1135–1204] says, we simply can have no idea of what pure spiritual bliss in the Hereafter is like. Agnosticism on the basic issue of whether there is a Hereafter would seem narrowness of vision believing what we do of God. But once the basic affirmation is made, it is almost as narrow to project our poor, early imaginings on the landscape of Heaven.[14]

In Summary

Throughout history, human beings have tried to unravel the mystery of death and to imagine what lies beyond the grave. Though some, including a handful of Jewish thinkers, have argued that the hope for immortality is a childish aspiration based on wish fulfillment, others reserve their judgment and prefer to leave this question unanswered, probably never to be resolved by a human being.

NOTES

1. *Gates of Prayer* (New York: Central Conference of American Rabbis [hereafter referred to as CCAR], 1975), p. 624.
2. Roland B. Gittelsohn, *Wings of the Morning* (New York: Union of American Hebrew Congregations [hereafter referred to as UAHC], 1969), p. 362.
3. *Gates of Repentance* (New York: CCAR, 1978), p. 484.
4. Maurice Lamm, *The Jewish Way in Death and Mourning* (New York: Jonathan David Publishers, 1969), p. xi.
5. Joshua L. Liebman, *Peace of Mind* (New York: Bantam Books, 1961), p. 106.
6. Quoted in *Rabbi's Manual* (New York: CCAR, 1988), p. 140.
7. Gittelsohn, *Wings,* pp. 347–48.
8. *Selected Essays of Ahad Ha-Am* (New York: Meridian Books, 1962), p. 84.
9. Ibid., p. 144.
10. Sigmund Freud, *The Future of an Illusion* (New York: Anchor Books, 1964), p. 54.
11. Ibid., pp. 77–78.
12. Richard L. Rubenstein, "The Making of a Rabbi," ed. I. Eisenstein, *Varieties of Jewish Belief* (New York: Reconstructionist Press, 1966), p. 179.
13. Ibid., pp. 194–95. For a similar view see Alvin Reines, Chapter Twelve of this book.
14. Louis Jacobs, *A Jewish Theology* (New York: Behrman House, 1973), p. 321.

· 2 ·

Down to Sheol

The people of the ancient Near East entertained a plethora of beliefs about the hereafter. These ideas, however, were rarely presented in a systematic fashion, generally appearing either in literary texts or in burial methods and mourning customs.

In the prevailing Mesopotamian and Canaanite mythologies, the universe was divided into three levels: the heavens, which were the domain of the "high" gods; the earth, which was given to humans, animals, plants, and inanimate objects; and the lower sphere, conceived as a gigantic cave, which housed the dead as well as some of the gods.

Ancestor worship was an important component of religious life. Human beings on earth were believed to be in constant communication with both the upper and lower realms. Public rituals and prayers were directed to the heavenly gods, while individual pleas were addressed to the inhabitants of the netherworld.

The Egyptians

The ancient Egyptians did not view death as an end to human life but as a new kind of living, provided the remains of the deceased were appropriately prepared and preserved. For example, the dead were entombed with food and drink, anointed with cosmetics and various oils, and buried with jewelry, clothing, and even weapons, supposedly to protect them from their enemies. The Egyptians believed that in the next world each person survived in both body and soul. To enable the body to recognize its earthly soul, the

Egyptians developed the art of mummification, the preservation of the body through a unique embalming process. Once these steps were taken, the ancient Egyptians maintained that the dead continued to live in the hereafter, following the daily routines of their lives: plowing, sowing, eating, and drinking.

The Babylonians

For the Babylonians, the realm of the dead was a dreary realm ruled by a ruthless divine king and queen—Ereshkigal and Nergal. In order to enter this "Land of No Return," one had to pass through seven gates. This realm is described vividly in a classic text. When Ishtar, the goddess of fertility, entered the netherworld, she came:

> To the dark house . . .
> To the house which none leave who have
>   entered it,
> To the road from which there is no way
>   back,
> To the house wherein the entrants are bereft
>   of light,
> Where dust is their fare and clay their food.
> [Where] they see no light, residing in darkness,
> [Where] they are clothed like birds, with
>   wings for garments,
> [And where] over door and bolt is spread
>   dust.[1]

The Biblical Israelites

Like other peoples in the ancient Near East, the Israelites held various conceptions of a hereafter.[2] The Tanach—the Torah, Prophets, and Writings—demonstrates an evolving understanding of life after death.

The Israelites were influenced more by the beliefs of the neighboring Babylonians than by the Egyptians. In considering the netherworld as a place of darkness, for example, they seem to have rejected the optimistic Egyptian belief in a physical existence after death.

The Israelites, however, did not subscribe blindly to Babylonian ideas, preferring to shape their own view of life after death. They considered the Canaanite custom of making inquiries of the dead an abomination (Deut. 18:11) and rejected the offering of sacrifices to the dead (Ps. 106:28; cf. Num. 25:2–3; Deut. 26:14). While there was no single biblical view of the afterlife, certain themes reoccurred, forming a framework of ancient beliefs and values. Two basic ideas seemed to dominate biblical thinking on life and death:

1. God is life-affirming and the source of all goodness. One finds in the Hebrew Scriptures few speculations about life after death and little preoccupation with the hereafter. The ultimate purpose is to "sanctify" life here on earth.

2. Death does not represent a total annihilation of the individual but a transition to a new kind of life, where people meet their own ancestors, continuing to live a shadowy kind of existence. This belief is reflected in the biblical saying that when one dies, one "goes" to one's "fathers" [ancestors] (see Gen. 15:15), or is "gathered to [one's] kin" (Gen. 25:8, 17).

Body and Soul Are One

Influenced by Greek philosophy, many of us speak about the "body" and "soul" as separate entities. The ancient Israelites made no such distinction, referring to a person, living or dead, as a *nefesh,* Hebrew for "soul," or "living being" (see Lev. 5:17; Num. 6:6). In other words, body and soul are one in life and in death.

Death Is the End of Physical Existence

In the Bible, death occurs for two basic reasons:

1. As a natural end of human life.
2. As a result of sin.

We live seventy years, or at most eighty (Ps. 90:10). (Gen. 6:3 puts the length of human life at 120 years.) After that we return to the soil from which we came. Just as we are born, so must we die in due time. This is made clear in various biblical passages:

> Dust you are, and to dust you shall return. (Gen. 3:19)

> In respect of the fate of man and the fate of beast, they have one and the same fate. . . . Both go to the same place; both came from dust and both return to dust. (Eccles. 3:19–20)

> We must all die; we are like water that is poured out on the ground and cannot be gathered up. (II Sam. 14:14)

We Can Feel the Presence of Death in Life

The Hebrew Bible implies that the power of death can invade the sphere of human life, there spreading its influence. The line between death and life is not clear-cut. A sick or injured person was often deemed to be in the hold of death, as we learn from the Psalmist: "Have mercy on me, O Lord; see my affliction at the hands of my foes, You who lift me from the gates of death" (9:14).

Good Deeds Can Extend Life

A number of passages in the Bible, including the fifth of the Ten Commandments, indicate that observing God's laws and commandments may lengthen one's days. In Exodus we read that people who honor their parents will "long endure on the land" God gives them (20:12). A law in the book of Deuteronomy states that if you happen to see a bird's nest with a mother bird laying eggs, you must first let the mother go before taking the eggs. If you do so, then you will "fare well and have a long life" (Deut. 22:7). Similarly a passage in Proverbs asserts that one "who spurns ill-gotten gains will live long" (28:16).

Sin Can Shorten Life

If long life was considered a reward, untimely death often was interpreted as divine punishment, as the following passages demonstrate:

> You surround them [the wicked] with flattery;
> You make them fall through blandishments.
> How suddenly are they ruined, wholly swept away by terrors.
> (Ps. 73:18–19)

> The joy of the wicked has been brief. . . .
> He perishes forever . . .   (Zophar in Job 20:5–7)

The Book of Genesis tells us that, at the instigation of Eve, Adam ate from the tree of knowledge. God was displeased that a divine order was ignored and established toil and death as a punishment. God said to Adam:

> By the sweat of your brow
> Shall you get bread to eat,
> Until you return to the ground.   (Gen. 3:19)

Fearful that Adam might also eat of the tree of life and thus become immortal, God took drastic measures: "[God] drove the man out, and stationed east of the garden of Eden the cherubim and the fiery ever-turning sword, to guard the way to the tree of life" (Gen. 3:24).

Sheol: A Mysterious Hint of a Life Beyond

The overwhelming message of the Bible is that death is final. After death, one is not expected to return to this earth. This teaching was dramatized by King David, who, after the death of his beloved son, bathed and anointed himself and asked that he be served food. His courtiers were surprised by this change of attitude. They said: "While the child was alive, you fasted and wept; but now that the child is dead, you rise and take food! He replied, ". . . But now that he is dead, why should I fast? Can I bring him back again? I shall go to him, but he will never come back to me" (II Sam. 12:23). The same idea was highlighted by Job when he said "If a man dies, can he live again?" (Job 14:14). The biblical answer is no.

Yet the ancient Israelites did not fully accept the notion of a total dissolution; rather, they spoke of a place called Sheol, where the dead dwell.[3]

Though the etymology of the word *Sheol* is unclear, in the Bible it always appears in the feminine form without a definite article, indicating that it is a proper noun. Some scholars argue that the term derives from the root "to call," suggesting Sheol is "a place of inquiry." Others argue that it is taken from another root meaning "hollow hand," suggesting Sheol is a "hollow place."

The Bible refers to Sheol as "the Ditch," "the Pit," "the realm of Death," "Perdition," "the Grave," "the Dust," "the torrents of Belial," and "the land of Darkness," among other things.

Whatever its original meaning, in the biblical understanding of the word, Sheol is a place located beneath the earth, a place to which one always "goes down." "To go down to Sheol," in the Hebrew, means "to die" (e.g., Gen. 37:35; 42:38). While a number of biblical passages refer to Sheol, two later texts venture a fuller imaginary description. In Isaiah 14:9–11, we find a song of scorn directed at the king of Babylon:

> Sheol below was astir
> To greet your coming —
> Rousing for you the shades
> Of all earth's chieftains,
> Raising from their thrones
> All the kings of nations.
> All speak up and say to you,
> "So you have been stricken as we were,
> You have become like us!
> Your pomp is brought down to Sheol,
> And the strains of your lutes!
> Worms are to be your bed,
> Maggots your blanket!"

In Psalms 88:4–7, the poet cries out:

> I am sated with misfortune;
> I am at the brink of Sheol.
> I am numbered with those who go down to the Pit;
> I am a helpless man
> abandoned among the dead,
> like bodies lying in the grave
> of whom You are mindful no more,
> and who are cut off from Your care.
> You have put me at the bottom of the Pit,
> in the darkest places, in the depths.

In other texts, Sheol is viewed as being somewhere beneath the waters (Job 26:5) or the earth (Num. 16:30; Ezek. 31:14; Ps. 88:7; Lam. 3:55), or at the base of high mountains (Jon. 2:7). This is not only a place of darkness (Ps. 88:13; Job 10:21–22) but also of silence (Ps. 115:17) enclosed by barred gates (Isa. 38:10; Job 38:17).

That Sheol is a land of no return is affirmed by Job: "As a cloud fades away,/So whoever goes down to Sheol does not come up" (7:9).

In Sheol, the dead cannot reach out to God. As the Psalmist cries out in distress:

> The dead cannot praise the Lord,
> nor any who go down into silence.   (115:17)

> There is no praise of You among the dead;
> in Sheol, who can acclaim you?   (6:6)

> For it is not Sheol that praises you,
> Not [the Land of] Death that extols You;
> Nor do they who descend into the Pit
> Hope for Your grace.   (Isa. 38:18)

In Sheol, however, the dead do not seem to disappear totally. A number of biblical texts clearly portray Sheol as the seat of a shadowy kind of existence. Very often the dead are referred to as *refaim* (shades): (see Ps. 88:11; Prov. 9:18; Job 26:5). They "chirp" (Isa. 29:4; cf. 8:19). They are "without strength" (Ps. 88:5) and "freed from the sickness of the flesh" (Job 3:17). God can hear their voices (Jon. 2:3). They maintain their earthly status even in this place of darkness. Chieftains "are raised from their thrones" (Isa. 14:9). Prophets keep their clothing (I Sam. 28:14). Though the dead do not praise God, God still has power over Sheol and can draw out those who are worthy (Ps. 30:4; 49:16; 116:8; 139:8).

Though dreary, Sheol is not seen as a place of punishment. Every living being, without regard to moral character, goes down to Sheol at the time of death (Ezek. 32:18–32; Job 3:17–19; Eccles. 3:19ff.). The concept of "hell," we shall see, developed in Israel much later during the Hellenistic period, probably under the influence of ancient Persian ideas.

There Is Life Beyond the Grave

Our study thus far reveals how the biblical Israelites struggled with the question of an afterlife. On the one hand, they affirmed the finality of death. On the other, they resisted the notion that the dead turned to dust. In two remarkable passages in the Bible we read that some people never died. For example, we are told that "Enoch walked with God; then he was no more, for God took him" (Gen. 5:24). Another text relates that the prophet "Elijah went up to heaven in a whirlwind" (II Kings 2:11).

In addition to these two enigmatic sections, we find a few biblical texts that actually speak of a return to earth. We are told, for example, that each of two legendary prophets, Elijah (I Kings 17:17–24) and Elisha (II Kings 4:17–37), revived a dead child. Another story relates: "Once . . . a man was being buried, when the people caught sight of such a band [the Moabites]; so they threw the corpse into Elisha's grave and made off. When the [dead] man came in contact with Elisha's bones, he came to life and stood up" (II Kings 13:21).

Belief in an afterlife also can be inferred from an examination of certain biblical laws. Societies promulgate laws to prohibit actions deemed disruptive or dangerous. Current laws against drunk driving, for example, would not have been enacted unless the problem was widespread.

The Bible prohibits necromancy—foretelling the future by communication with the dead. The Book of Deuteronomy states: "Let no one be found among you . . . who casts spells or . . . consults ghosts or familiar spirits or . . . inquires of the dead" (18:10–11; cf. Lev. 19:31).

The very existence of this law suggests the widespread practice of casting spells, consulting ghosts and spirits, and inquiring of the dead. Indeed, other biblical references support this assumption. At times, people did "inquire of the ghosts and familiar spirits that chirp and moan" (Isa. 8:19). King Manasseh of Judah "practiced soothsaying, divination, and sorcery, and consulted ghosts and familiar spirits" (II Chron. 33:6).

In response, King Josiah of Judah "did away with the necromancers and the mediums" (II Kings 23:24). Before him, King Saul banned the use of ghosts and familiar spirits in the land (see I Sam. 28:9). But even Saul felt compelled to violate his own law and contacted the famous witch of En-dor. When the Philistine army threatened to defeat him, Saul prayed to God for guidance. When God did not "answer," Saul forced the woman of En-dor to raise up the prophet Samuel from his grave.

> And the woman said to Saul: "I see a divine being coming up from the earth." "What does he look like?" he asked her. "It is an old man coming up," she said, "and he is wrapped up in a robe." Then Saul knew that it was Samuel; and he bowed low in homage with his face to the ground.
>
> Samuel said to Saul, "Why have you disturbed me and brought me up?" And Saul answered, "I am in great trouble. . . ."
>
> (I Sam. 28:13–15)

In short, belief in an afterlife had strong appeal in the biblical world. God, who had power over Sheol and could rescue the individual from the Pit, was believed to possess the power to revive the dead, individually or collectively.

The Canaanites, who cohabited the land, spoke confidently about their gods, who died and rose up again. Other surrounding peoples, notably the Persians, believed with conviction in a physical afterlife. In fact, Zoroaster, the ancient Persian prophet who lived around 500 B.C.E., already predicted a general resurrection of the dead as part of an ultimate purification of the earth. All of these influences contributed to the changing perception of life beyond the grave in Jewish thought.

Seeds of a Belief in Resurrection

The first clear notion of resurrection in Judaism appears in the writings of the prophet Ezekiel. Following the destruction of Jerusalem by the Babylonians in 586 B.C.E., this great prophet of the Exile dreamed of a time when the Israelite nation would be restored. Ezekiel described his vision of being taken by God to a valley of bones.

> And He said to me: O mortal, these bones are the whole House of Israel. They say, "Our bones are dried up, our hope is gone; we are doomed." Prophesy, therefore, and say to them: Thus said the Lord God: I am going to open your graves and lift you out of the graves, O My people, and bring you to the land of Israel. (Ezek. 37:11–12)

In this prophecy there is no indication of a belief in *personal* resurrection. Rather, the prophet, using poetic imagery, speaks of the restoration of *national* life.

In the book of Daniel, however, written about the second century B.C.E., there can be no doubt of the author's message: "Many of those that sleep in the dust of the earth will awake, some to eternal life, others to reproaches, to everlasting abhorrence" (12:2; cf. Isa. 25:8; 26:19).

Yet even in this text resurrection is not universal but restricted to a limited few (viz. "many of those . . ."). In the Exilic period (sixth to fifth century B.C.E.), while the doctrine of the final disposition of those resurrected from the earth was not yet crystallized, a belief in bodily resurrection was already established, an idea that was to become a fundamental tenet of Judaism during the rabbinic period.

In Summary

The ancient Israelites borrowed concepts of the afterlife from surrounding cultures, adapting and refining them; for them, death was not the end but rather a transition to another kind of shadowy life in Sheol. Good deeds were thought to extend life while sins shortened it.

The biblical view of what lies beyond the grave ranges from the netherworld of Sheol to a rudimentary belief in personal resurrection.

NOTES

1. James B. Pritchard, ed., "Descent of Ishtar to the Netherworld," *Ancient Near Eastern Texts Relating to the Old Testament* [hereafter referred to as *ANET*] (Princeton, N.J.: Princeton University Press, 3rd ed., 1969), p. 107.

2. For the biblical concepts of afterlife see Bernhard Lang, "Afterlife: Ancient Israel's Changing Vision of the World Beyond," *Bible Review*, February 1988, pp. 12–23. Also see Helmer Ringgren, *Israelite Religion* (Philadelphia: Fortress Press, 1966), pp. 239–47.

3. On this term, see "Dead, Abode of the," *The Interpreter's Dictionary of the Bible*, Vol. 1 (New York; Nashville, Tenn.: Abingdon Press, 1962), pp. 787–88.

· 3 ·

Resurrection
of the Body and Soul,
Hell and Paradise

The Meaning of Resurrection

People of many faiths believe that in the distant future the dead will be "resurrected," i.e., they will come back to life. The term "resurrection" comes from Latin and means "to rise again." In most religious systems, resurrection is tied to a vision of "the end of days," when the dead will rise from their graves. This notion evolved through the ages in Jewish thought and later influenced Christianity and Islam.

A Cardinal Belief

Belief in the resurrection of the body and soul emerged as a basic "dogma" of rabbinic Judaism. Two major Jewish "sects," the Pharisees and Sadducees, bitterly debated the issue as recorded by the first-century Jewish historian Josephus. The Pharisees said:

> Souls have an immortal vigor in them. . . . Under the earth there will be rewards and punishments according as they have lived virtuously or viciously in this life. . . . The latter are to be detained in an everlasting prison. . . . The former shall have power to revive and live again.

The Sadducees, on the other hand, argued that "souls die with the bodies."[1]

21

While we do not know when Jews were first exposed to the notion of resurrection, Louis Jacobs asserts that the doctrine of the hereafter came into full prominence among Jews during the Maccabean period (about the second century B.C.E.) when many good people were dying for their faith and the older view of reward and punishment in this life was becoming untenable. From this time on, the belief in resurrection was so firmly established, the rabbis began to argue, sometimes fancifully, that the idea was clearly evident in the Hebrew Bible.

> Rabbi Meir said: Where can we see that resurrection is derived from the Torah? In the passage: "Then will Moses and the children of Israel sing this song to the Lord" (Exod. 15:1). It does not say "sang" (past tense) but "*will* sing" (future). Therefore, resurrection is deducible from the Torah. Again, Rabbi Joshua B. Levi asked: "Where can we see that resurrection is derived from the Torah? In the passage 'Happy are those who dwell in Your house, they will be still praising you' (Ps. 84:5), it is not stated 'they *have* praised You' but '*will be* praising You' [in the hereafter]; therefore, resurrection is derived from the Torah (i.e., Psalms)." (*San.* 91b)

In time, the arguments of the Sadducees were rejected, and the Pharisaic belief in resurrection became an unchallenged "dogma" of Judaism. To reinforce this credo, the rabbis identified those who would be denied this great blessing:

> All Israelites have a share in the world to come. . . . [However], these are they that have no share in the world to come [in spite of the fact that they are Israelites]: one who says there is no resurrection of the dead prescribed in the Torah, and [one who says] that the Torah is not from Heaven [i.e., divinely revealed], and an Epicurean [maybe one who denies divine providence and retribution in this life and the other].
> (*San.* 10:1)

Other rabbis added their own list. For example, Rabbi Akiba said: "[Resurrection will be denied to] one who reads heretical books or utters charms over a wound [i.e., magic]." Rabbi Saul professed it would also be denied to "one who pronounced God's name with its proper letters [i.e., as it appears in the text, which is prohibited]."[2]

This phenomenon, making ultimate salvation conditional upon belief, represented a radical break with the Jewish past. Until now, actions alone determined eligibility for God's favor or liability for divine punishment. Time and time again the Israelites were told all would be well "if you observe the laws and commandments, the statutes and ordinances, that the Lord your God has commanded you."

Now belief became as important as deed, so central was the former's role in the Judaism of the era. To question resurrection was to forfeit eternal life.

Problem of Terminology

In his classic work on Rabbinic Judaism, J. F. Moore states: "Any attempt to systemize the Jewish notions of the hereafter imposes upon them an order and consistency which does not exist in them."[3]

Though the rabbis staunchly defended a belief in resurrection of body and soul, they tolerated a great deal of speculation as to how it would occur and what lay beyond the grave. The terminology they used was quite ambiguous and changed over time. By the end of the talmudic period and into the Middle Ages, however, the rabbis arrived at a standard series of terms that they used to discuss the hereafter.

They called the world in which we live *haolam hazeh* (this world) and the hereafter *haolam haba* (the world to come), or *atid lavo* (what is to come). In their view, the transition from one world to the next begins with the termination of human life on earth and includes at least two major components: Messianic Times and Resurrection and Final Judgment.

Messianic Times

The Hebrew word for messiah, *mashiach,* means "anointed." In biblical times, prophets, priests, and kings were anointed to indicate their special status in society. Many cultic objects, such as altars, pillars, and arks were also consecrated through an anointing ceremony. The very idea of a "messianic king" was projected back to David, king of Israel. When David's son Solomon died, the kingdom split into two parts. Rehoboam, Solomon's son, ruled the southern kingdom of Judah, and the rebel Jeroboam reigned over Israel in the north. Soon after, the Assyrians defeated Israel (in 722–21 B.C.E.) and led the ten northern tribes into exile.

Afterward a dream was born: One day, in the distant future, a descendant of King David would arise and gather in Israel all the lost tribes, restoring them to their glorious past. With it would come an age of tranquillity and peace for all humanity. As Maimonides, the great medieval Jewish scholar, writes: "In that era there will be neither famine nor war, neither jealousy nor strife. Blessings will be abundant, comforts within the reach of all" (*Mishneh Torah*, Kings 12:5).[4]

Our rabbinic sages looked forward to this blessed time but did not formulate normative teachings about its realization. In fact, various scenarios were advanced regarding this great happening. One the one hand, some talmudic statements indicated that during the days of the Messiah miraculous things would occur, such as one olive feeding a great many people and one grape producing wine for a multitude. On the other hand, however, some rabbis stripped the messianic times of all supernatural overtones. Thus, said one sage: "The sole difference between the present and the messianic days is delivery from servitude to foreign powers" (*Ber.* 34b; cf. *San.* 91b). Maimonides added: "Do not think that King Messiah will have to perform signs and wonders, bring anything new into being, revive the dead, or do similar things. It is not so" (*Mishneh Torah,* Kings 11:3).

Yet most rabbis were aware of the difference between the messianic times and the days of the world to come. Rabbi Johannan said: "Every prophet prophesied only for the days of the Messiah; but as for the World to Come, no eye has seen what God has prepared for those who wait for Him" (*Ber.* 34b).

Resurrection—Final Judgment

Concepts of hell and paradise are well established in rabbinic literature, though there is a great diversity of theological detail.

It was generally accepted that in the world to come *(haolam haba)*, the righteous would be rewarded and the wicked punished. The rabbis taught that the former would go to paradise (in Hebrew, *Gan Eden*, the Garden of Eden) and the latter to hell (in Hebrew, *gehinnom*, Gehenna). Beyond these basic tenets, however, individual rabbis offered imaginative scenarios. Some sages argued that the righteous and the wicked would go to their respective places only after resurrection and final judgment. Others maintained that the departed would assume their assigned locations immediately following death. Some asserted that the soul would remain with the body for a brief period (three days, seven days, twelve months, etc.) and then ascend. Others declared that after death the soul returns to a heavenly "treasury" and waits there until the period of resurrection.

Who Goes Where?

Who enters *haolam haba*? The basic Jewish view, as stated earlier, is that "all Israelites have a share in the world to come," with some exceptions *(San.* 10:1). In an attempt to promote an exemplary way of life, a number of rabbis argued that certain behaviors or actions assured one of a "share in the world to come." Studying Torah, living in Israel, getting married, leading others to do good, and speaking Hebrew were only a few of the certain paths to immortal life. On the other hand, those who exalted themselves at the expense of others, studied secular literature, or engaged in magic, or even sang the Song of Songs in a tavern to a popular tune risked losing their place in *haolam haba*.

In some cases, in order to justify the unknown ways of God, the rabbis promised a place in the world to come to the poor or suffering on earth. To others it was denied on theological grounds, i.e., whoever said that resurrection of the dead was not indicated in the Torah or that the Torah was not of divine origin (see *San.* 10:1).

As to the fate of non-Jews, the rabbis of the second century differed sharply. One rabbi, taking a minority view, argued that gentiles do not have any place in the world to come. The position of another sage, Rabbi Joshua ben Hananiah, prevailed: "Righteous gentiles have a place in the world to come" (*Tos. San.* 13:2). This view was also affirmed by the great medieval philosopher and legal scholar Maimonides, who stated: "The pious of all the nations of the world have a portion in the world to come" (*Mishneh Torah,* Repentance 3:5).

What Is Hell (Gehinnom) *Like?*

The term "Gehenna" dates from the biblical period and refers to a valley south of Jerusalem called *Ge Ben Hinnom.* In ancient times, the valley was the site of a heathen cult whose rituals included the burning of children (see II Kings 23:10; Jer. 7:31). In the rabbinic period, it was conceived of as a site of torment for the wicked after death, a place so vast that it was compared to a pot whose lid was formed by the rest of the universe (see *Pes.* 94a).

Gehenna was seen primarily as a place of punishment and purgation. According to one opinion in the Talmud:

> Wrongdoers of Israel who sin with their body, and wrongdoers of the gentiles who sin with their body, go to *Gehinnom* and are punished there for twelve months. After twelve months their body is consumed and their soul is burned and the wind scatters them under the soles of the feet of the righteous.
>
> [*R.H.* 17a)

Though some sages argued that the wicked would be annihilated forever, Rabbi Akiba taught that "the judgment of the wicked in Gehenna shall endure [only] twelve months" (*Ed.* 2:10). After one year, taught Akiba, even the wicked would be returned to paradise. Ultimately the position of Akiba held sway.

The rabbis were aware that the majority of people were neither totally righteous nor completely wicked. Most people fell between the two extremes, not righteous enough to enter paradise at once but not evil enough to merit the fires of hell. Thus the question arose: Where do these people go?

The competing schools of two great Jewish teachers, Hillel and Shammai, debated this issue. The school of Shammai said:

> There will be three groups on the Day of Judgment: one of thoroughly righteous people, one of thoroughly wicked people, and one of people in between. The first group will be inscribed for everlasting life; the second group will be doomed in Gehinnom [forever] . . . the third will go down to Gehinnom and squeal and rise again [to be healed].   [*R.H.* 16b–17a)

The more tolerant school of Hillel, on the other hand, argued that God would be merciful, give those "in between" the benefit of the doubt, and thus send them to paradise rather than to Gehenna on the Day of Judgment. But Rabbi Hanina taught that all who go down to hell will go up again, except the following: the adulterer, one who puts his fellow to shame in public, and one who calls his fellow by an obnoxious nickname (see *B.M.* 58b).

In describing Gehenna, writers often have given free rein to their fantasies. No description, however, is as vivid and detailed as that of Immanuel ben Solomon of Rome (born about 1270). Immanuel, a contemporary of Dante, wrote a book entitled *Tophet and Eden* (Hell and Paradise) in much the same style as Dante's *Divine Comedy*. Immanuel narrates an imaginary dream in which he visits the places of human destiny.

On the fate of the wicked, he wrote:

> We journeyed thence, and lo, there were pits full of serpents, poisonous and flying, hundreds and thousands of lions and leopards were dying, and round about angels of death with their swords were plying, and torrents of mighty waters in floods were lying, making the hearts of onlookers gasp with sighing.

Then said I, Who are these that for destruction are eagerly trying? He replied, These be they caught in witchcraft and divining, necromancers, and magicians . . .[5]

In another scene:

And as we journeyed thence, we saw a man with his right hand and tongue all slit; they had made of him a target, against which with darts from brazen bow they hit, so that thereby to the earth his very gall, pouring forth, did flit. Now, placed upon an iron grid, he would of roasting endure the pang; again, in bitter waters they would immerse him with a clang; then again, him upon a wooden gallows they would hang; at another time with stones at him they would bang. Then I asked the man who spake with me, Why this situation, what the cause and reason for this special tribulation?

And he replied and said: His was a tongue that did speak vauntingly, and in his heart iniquity did ramble jauntingly.[6]

This frightening description of hell sought to convince people of the terrible consequences of wicked acts on earth.

What Is Paradise (Gan Eden) *Like?*

The word "paradise" is the English derivative of the Greek word for garden and refers to the Garden of Eden planted by God for Adam and Eve (see Gen. 2–3). In the Bible the Garden of Eden is an earthly place. By rabbinic times, it had become identified as the abode of the righteous after death. In fact, the rabbis speak of two different gardens of Eden: a) the earthly, with abundant vegetation and fertility; and b) the heavenly, as the habitation for the righteous.

Neither location is known. According to the rabbis, God will reveal to Israel the path to Eden during the messianic period.

Beginning with the rabbinic period, paradise has been viewed by Jews as a place of bliss and blessing but imagined in a variety of ways, often personally revealing. One sage, for example, maintained that three things—namely, Shabbat, sunshine, and sexual intercourse are central in this world as well as in the world to come (see *Ber.* 57b).

He was not alone in viewing paradise as a sensual place. We read that the righteous will sit at golden tables (*Ta'an.* 25a) on stools of gold (*Ket.* 77b) and participate in lavish banquets (*B.B.* 75a). A third-century Babylonian scholar, Rav, disagreed:

> In the world to come there is neither eating nor drinking; no procreation of children or business transactions, no envy or hatred or rivalry; but the righteous sit enthroned, their crowns on their heads, and enjoy the luster of the Shechinah (divine grace).   (*Ber.* 17a)

One of the most colorful descriptions of paradise, as one might expect, was penned by Immanuel ben Solomon of Rome. In one of the scenes, Immanuel says:

> Tables and candlesticks, thrones and crowns were there to be seen; they were for the souls that were pure and clean; and there was a throne of ivory, great in size, overlaid with gold in wealth, giving life unto those who reached it, and unto their flesh giving health; and the stones of a crown shone forth upon it on high; while garments of blue and purple and scarlet were spread, and about it did lay like polished copper gleaming, unto all lands their beauty beaming.[7]

Paradise for the rabbis was primarily a place of reward. Even though there were some who argued, like Rabbi Jacob, that "there is no reward for precepts in this world" (*Kid.* 39b), the majority of the sages seem to have agreed with Rabbi Tarfon, who taught: "You know that the bestowal of reward upon the righteous will be in the time to come" (*Avot* 2:16), in paradise.

Bodily Resurrection

According to the dominant rabbinic view, physical resurrection of the dead would take place at the end of time after the arrival of the Messiah. Rabbi Eleazar Ha-Kappar taught: "They that are

What Happens After I Die?

born [are destined] to die; and the dead [are destined] to be brought to life again; and the living [i.e., the resurrected] [are destined] after death to be judged" (*Avot* 4:28).

The rabbis maintained that both body and soul would be brought back to life and jointly subjected to the final judgment. R. Ishmael said:

> This may be compared to the case of a king who had an orchard containing excellent early figs, and he placed there two watchmen, one lame and the other blind. He said to them: "Be careful with these fine early figs." After some days the lame man said to the blind one: "I see fine early figs in the orchard." Said the blind man to him: "Come let us eat them." "Am I then able to walk?" said the lame man. "Can I then see?" retorted the blind man. The lame man got astride the blind man, and thus they ate the early figs and sat down again each in his place. After some days the king came into that vineyard and said to them: "Where are the fine early figs?" The blind man replied: 'My lord the king, can I then see?" The lame man replied: "My lord the king, can I then walk?" What did the king, who was a man of insight, do with them? He placed the lame man astride the blind man, and they began to move about. Said the king to them: "Thus have you done, and eaten the early figs." Even so will the Holy One, blessed be He, in the time to come, say to the soul: "Why hast thou sinned before Me?" and the soul will answer: "O Master of the universe, it is not I that sinned, but the body it is that sinned. Why, since leaving it, I am like a clean bird flying through the air. As for me, how have I sinned?" God will also say to the body: "Why hast thou sinned before Me?" and the body will reply: "O Master of the universe, not I have sinned, the soul it is that has sinned. Why, since it left me, I am cast about like a stone thrown upon the ground. Have I then sinned before Thee?" What will the Holy One, blessed be He, do to them? He will bring the soul and force it into the body, and judge both as one.
>
> (*Lev. Rabbah* 4:5, Soncino)

Is Resurrection Possible? And How?

The sages of the rabbinic period and many of the medieval Jewish scholars who affirmed belief in bodily resurrection did not have a problem fathoming resurrection because they already believed in God's omnipotence and creation ex nihilo (i.e., that the universe was created out of nothing). If God could create the world out of nothing, God could very well arrange it so that bodies and souls would be united miraculously at the time of resurrection. The Jewish philosopher Hasdai ben Abraham Crescas (1340–1410) even argued that God could create a body exactly like that which had lived on earth, endow it with the old soul, and keep it in storage for the time of retribution.

How will this resurrection take place? The ancient sages had some answers for this. For example: "As a man goes, so he returns. If he died blind or deaf or lame, he lives again blind or deaf or lame."[8]

Another opinion was: "Rabbi Hiyya ben Joseph said: A time will come when the just will break through [the soil] and rise up in Jerusalem. . . . He further stated: The just in the time to come will rise [dressed] in their clothes (*Ket.* 111b).

Some practical questions were raised by a Babylonian scholar, Saadia ben Yosef al-Fayyumi (892–942), head of the famous Sura Rabbinic Academy. In his major study, *The Book of Beliefs and Opinions,* he discusses a number of hypothetical situations:

> Suppose a lion were to eat a man, and then the lion would drown and a fish would eat him up, and then the fish would be caught and a man would eat him, and then the man would be burned and turned into ashes. Whence would the Creator restore the first man? Would He do it from the lion or the fish or the second man or the fire or the ashes?[9]

His answer: The parts of the body are kept aside by God and not mixed with others. They remain separate until the time of resurrection.

Another question: "Will these individuals who are destined to be resurrected in this world eat and drink and marry, or will they not do any of these things?"[10] The answer: They will eat and drink as we do; they will also marry.

Again, "In the case in which those to be resurrected were married while they were alive in this world, will each man's wife return to him because of the fact that she had formerly lived with him, or does death dissolve all marital ties?"[11] Saadia does not have an answer to this difficult question. He states that "our minds are capable only of grasping our present state,"[12] and that at the time of resurrection "there will be available . . . prophets and prophetic inspiration and divine guidance."[13]

He also raises the question of space: Will there be room for all those resurrected? His answer is yes. There is plenty of room in this world for all of them.

Will the resurrected recognize their family members? Again, the answer is yes. Will those who died blemished be cured? In opposition to the early rabbinic opinion, he says yes. Finally, what will happen to those whose life is about to end at the time of redemption? Will they die at all? Saadia prefers one of many opinions on this subject and says that they will live a long time but will die in order to be resurrected with the rest of humanity.

The philosopher Saadia, and many like him, engaged in theological speculation about the mystery of resurrection not only because they believed in it but because they wanted to provide practical guidance to those who lived with that expectation. Faith in resurrection provided comfort, solace, and hope for many.

Modern Times

Even today many Jews believe in resurrection. Orthodox Jews affirm it in their daily prayers.

Moses Mendelssohn (1729–1786), the great Jewish thinker of the Enlightenment, flatly rejected the idea of Gehenna, saying it was incompatible with Judaism's belief in a merciful God. Early Reform Jews rejected the concept of hell and paradise. Abraham Geiger (1810–1874), one of the guiding forces of Reform Judaism in Germany, suggested that "From now on, the hope for an afterlife should not be expressed in terms which suggest a future revival, a resurrection of the body; rather, they must stress the immortality of the human soul."[14]

The Philadelphia Conference of American Reform Rabbis (1869) affirmed: "The belief in bodily resurrection has no religious foundation."[15]

The same idea was repeated in the 1885 Pittsburgh Platform of the Central Conference of American Rabbis: "We reject as ideas not rooted in Judaism the belief both in bodily resurrection and in Gehenna and Eden (hell and paradise) as abodes for everlasting punishment or reward."[16]

As a result of these teachings, the Reform Jewish prayer book changed the Orthodox blessing that speaks of God as one "who revives the dead" to "Praised be Thou, O Lord, who hast implanted within us eternal life."[17] In the new *Gates of Prayer*, the same prayer now reads: "Blessed is the Lord, the Source of life" (*mechayeh hakol*).[18] Even where the *Gates of Prayer* has the traditional wording, *mechayeh hametim*,[19] it is left untranslated and interpreted in terms of spiritual immortality.[20]

Among modern thinkers, Will Herberg argues in favor of the belief in resurrection. He writes:

> The symbol "resurrection of the dead" expresses the depth and dimensions of Hebraic religion in relation to the destiny of mankind more adequately perhaps than any other concept . . . it is a doctrine with which we cannot dispense . . .[21]

Similarly, a modern Orthodox rabbi, Maurice Lamm, writes:

> The belief in a bodily resurrection appears, at first sight, to be incredible to the contemporary mind. But when approached from the God's-eye view, why is rebirth more miraculous than birth? . . . Surely resurrection is not beyond the capacity of an omnipotent God.[22]

Though most Reform and Reconstructionist Jews have set aside a belief in bodily resurrection, a few Reform thinkers are willing to reconsider the issue. In an article in the *Journal of Reform Judaism*,[23] Rabbi Richard Levy argues that "if Reform has affirmed these ideas [the miracle of the Exodus and the notion that God 'rested' on Shabbat], which reason and nature would seem to contradict, why eliminate resurrection and other beliefs related to the messianic future? . . . Each morning's arising [is] a little resurrection." He maintains that Reform Jews should "rescue" this "embarrassing but profound belief," for *techiyat hametim* has at least three things to recommend it:

1. It is faithful to the nature of our being as creations of God.
2. It is compatible with the basic covenantal promise that has bound our people with God since the days of Abraham.
3. By its connection with the messianic promise, it binds us to *Eretz Yisrael* in a manner that political or cultural Zionism fails to do.[24]

In Summary

The belief in resurrection, held today by Orthodox and many Conservative Jews, was central to rabbinic Judaism but rejected by a major segment of the Jewish community during the period following the Enlightenment. Now it has once again surfaced among some liberal Jews, who affirm it with a sense of authenticity. A belief that brought great comfort to our ancestors continues to radiate hope in our generation.

NOTES

1. Flavius Josephus, *Antiquities,* xviii, 1:3,4; cf. *Wars,* ii, 8:14. *Complete Works,* trans. W. Whiston (Grand Rapids, Mich.: Kregel, 1963).
2. See also *San.* 10:2–4 for other examples.
3. J. F. Moore, *Judaism,* Vol. 2 (Cambridge, Mass.: Harvard University Press, 1962), p. 389.
4. Quoted in Isadore Twersky, *A Maimonides Reader* (New York: Behrman House, 1972), pp. 225–26.
5. Immanuel ben Solomon of Rome, *Tophet and Eden* (Hell and Paradise), trans. Hermann Gollancz (London: University of London, 1921), p. 46.
6. Ibid., p. 35.
7. Ibid., p. 6.
8. Quoted in Vayigash 8, Tanhuma, Montefiore and Loewe, *A Rabbinic Anthology* (Cleveland, Ohio; New York: Meridian Books, 1963), p. 593.
9. Saadia Gaon, *The Book of Beliefs and Opinions,* trans. Samuel Rosenblatt (New Haven, Conn.: Yale University Press, 1948), p. 278.

10. Ibid., p. 280.
11. Ibid., p. 282.
12. Ibid.
13. Ibid.
14. Quoted in W. Gunther Plaut, *The Rise of Reform Judaism* (New York: World Union for Progressive Judaism [hereafter referred to as WUPJ], 1963), p. 158.
15. Quoted in W. Gunther Plaut, *The Growth of Reform Judaism* (New York: WUPJ, 1965), p. 31.
16. Ibid., p. 34.
17. *Union Prayer Book,* Vol. 1 (New York: CCAR, 1940), p. 18.
18. *Gates of Prayer* (New York: CCAR, 1975), p. 135.
19. Ibid., p. 256.
20. See also *Gates of Repentance,* p. 400, where the wording is kept as *mechayeh hametim.*
21. Will Herberg, *Judaism and Modern Man* (New York: Harper and Row, 1965), p. 229.
22. Maurice Lamm, *The Jewish Way in Death and Mourning* (New York: Jonathan David, 1969), p. 230.
23. Richard Levy, "Upon Arising: An Affirmation of Techiyat Hameitim," *Journal of Reform Judaism,* CCAR, Fall 1982, 12–20.
24. Ibid., p. 14.

·4·

Immortality

What Is Immortality?

Throughout history many people have affirmed that after death even though our bodies waste away, something of ourselves remains. They have adhered to the belief that our soul, or intellect, or spirit does not disappear but returns to the Source of all life.

This theory cannot be confirmed empirically, but several thinkers have advanced compelling arguments. Some, for example, have argued that we are part of the entire universe and that whatever makes the universe "whole" is never totally lost. The Greek philosopher Plato proposed the idea that human souls are immortal because, he declared, they lived before they were united with their bodies. Surely if they lived *prior* to that, they would continue to live even after the body had decayed. Others have asserted that the idea of immortality is "psychologically constructive" and therefore should be embraced regardless of its truth. Indeed, the German philosopher Immanuel Kant maintained that moral justice in the universe *requires* immortality, for the idea of immortality as a reward for righteousness leads people to virtuous living.

Though none of these notions is conclusive, the fundamental hypothesis of the soul's immortality has for centuries fired the Jewish imagination. As one modern thinker, D. A. Wells, put it: "The belief in a future life has been one of those commitments which the eager assert without evidence yet with great emotional comfort."[1] The belief in immortality is most often asserted as a matter

36

of faith, with supporting arguments designed to strengthen that faith rather than to establish it.

Until Resurrection

The rabbinic view of the hereafter includes both resurrection of the body and the immortality of the soul.[2] The rabbis of the talmudic period taught that after death the soul "ascends." The body remains in the grave until God miraculously unites the body and soul for everlasting life. The rabbis argued, however, that even before reunification with their bodies, souls live independently in the heavens and are aware of their own existence.

We find references to the idea that the "soul" is separable from the body in many rabbinic texts, including a statement that "the souls which are yet to be born" live in the heavens (*Hag.* 12b).

In a comment on the biblical verse, "And He breathed into his [Adam's] nostrils" (Gen. 2:7), one rabbi states: "This teaches that He set him [Adam] up as a lifeless mass reaching from earth to heaven and then infused a soul into him" (*Gen. Rabbah* 14:8, Soncino, p. 116).

Similarly we are told that the soul "ascends and descends" (Ibid., 14:9), presumably during sleep, then leaves the body at death to be reunited with it at resurrection: "For a full twelve months the body is in existence, and the soul ascends and descends. After twelve months the body ceases to exist, and the soul ascends but does not descend anymore (*Shab.* 152b/153a, Soncino).

A number of talmudic passages describe the soul's existence after death and its awareness of its surroundings:

> Rabbi Abbahu said: The dead man knows all that is said in his presence until the top-stone closes [the grave]. Rabbi Hiyya and Rabbi Simeon B. Rabbi differ. One maintains [that the dead hear] until the top-stone closes [the grave]; the other says until the flesh rots away.　　(*Shab.* 152b, Soncino)

> Rabbi Eliezer said: The souls of the righteous are hidden under the Throne of Glory. . . . But those of the wicked continue

> to be imprisoned, while one angel stands at one end of the world, and a second stands at the other end, and they sling their souls to each other. . . .   (Ibid.)

In a remarkable talmudic text, we find two souls conversing with each other:

> It is related that a certain pious man gave a denar (coin) to a poor man on the eve of the New Year in a year of drought, and his wife scolded him, and he went and passed the night in the cemetery, and he heard two spirits conversing with each other. Said one [spirit] to her companion: My dear, come and let us wander about the world and let us hear from behind the curtain [Divine presence] what suffering is coming on the world. Said her companion to her: I am not able, because I am buried in a matting of reeds. But you go, and whatever you hear tell me. So the other went and wandered about and returned.   (*Ber.* 18b, Soncino)

Other passages allude to a separate existence of the soul from the body: "Is not the poor soul a guest in the body?" (*Lev. Rabbah* 34:3). "Just as God fills the world, sees but is not seen, so the soul fills the body, sees but is not seen" (*Ber.* 10a).

The idea of the soul's separation from the body after death was affirmed by many rabbis through the Middle Ages and beyond. Saadia ben Yosef al-Fayyumi concurred with the view that every person is endowed with a soul. He added, however, that this soul is created by God at the time when the human body is completed, and thus does not have a preexisting life. After death, the soul leaves for the world to come until resurrection when, together with the body, it will undergo a final judgment. Isaac Israeli (ca. 850–950) and Judah Halevi (born about 1080) advanced similar opinions. Yet there were other Jewish thinkers, particularly those influenced by Greek philosophy, who believed that the soul, but not the body, was immortal and that the soul would live but the body would decay.

Our Soul Alone Is Immortal

Resurrection of the body and the immortality of the soul are the two essential components of the rabbinic Jewish belief in the hereafter; the former was stressed among Jews in Palestine, the latter among Hellenistic Jews, such as Philo of Alexandria (20 B.C.E. to 50 C.E.).

Philo's major accomplishment was his synthesis of Judaism and Greek thought. He argued that Judaism could in large measure be understood and appreciated by Jews in terms of Greek philosophy. A disciple of the Greek philosopher Plato (427–347 B.C.E.), Philo taught that human beings are composed of body and soul, the body connecting us with matter and the soul linking us with God. Like other Greek thinkers of this time, Philo affirmed that the body is the source of evil in humans. The soul, on the other hand, and in particular the rational part of the soul, reflects the Divine. By uniting with the body, and thus with matter, the soul becomes vulnerable to evil. A major human goal, therefore, must be for individuals to rescue themselves from the evil of the body by subduing their passions and eliminating their sensuality. Philo believed that human souls are immortal: "Some of the souls have descended into bodies, but others have never deigned to be brought into union with any of the parts of the earth."[3]

In Philo's view, souls depart from earthly bodies after death and return to heaven, where they rejoin other souls (namely, angels), which never have entered bodies. Plato and Philo differed on a major point. Plato assumed the existence of a single universal soul. Philo, most likely influenced by his Jewish background, maintained that each soul remains independent, thus preserving the idea of immortality of the individual soul, in agreement with the rabbis of his time.

Philo never speaks of bodily resurrection. H. A. Wolfson pointed out:

> No direct or indirect reference to resurrection as distinguished from immortality is even made by him. . . . It is quite evident that all the references to resurrection . . . were understood by him as being only a figurative way of referring to immortality [of the soul].[4]

Philo pointed to heaven as the ultimate place for the righteous. But what of the wicked? Where were they destined to go? Philo responds: ". . . Awaiting those who live in the way [of the impious] will be eternal death."[5]

Another Jew who presumably lived in Hellenistic Alexandria around the time of Philo advanced a similar point of view. In a book entitled *The Wisdom of Solomon,* whose author and date of composition are unknown, we find the following lines:

> But the souls of the righteous are in the hand of God, and no torment will ever touch them. In the eyes of the foolish they seem to have died, and their departure was thought to be an affliction, and their going from us to be their destruction, but they are at peace.   (3:1–3, RSV)

Here, too, we find a clear reference to the immortality of the individual soul and a statement of faith that "immortality brings one near to God" (6:19, RSV).

All of these thinkers conceived of the soul as an independent component of human life. There were, however, other Jewish thinkers who spoke of the immortality of the "intellect" rather than the soul.

Our Intellect Alone Is Immortal

Many Greek philosophers, Aristotle among them, maintained that what lives on forever after death is our "intellect," which is "illuminated" by the light of the "universal intellect." To the extent that we develop our powers of reason, they posited, we can tune in to the universal intellect, which is endless or eternal.

One of the most prominent advocates of this idea in Judaism was Maimonides, who was influenced by Aristotle. Maimonides did not clearly declare his personal belief, since to do so would have been heretical in his time. Instead, he concealed his real intentions, using ambiguous terminology and contradictory or "equivocal" phrases. In his Commentary to the *Mishneh,* Maimonides states:

> The resurrection of the dead is one of the cardinal principles established by Moses our Teacher. A person who does not

believe in this principle has no real religion, certainly not Judaism. However, resurrection is only for the righteous.[6]

Maimonides includes the belief in resurrection as one of the Thirteen Principles of Faith, although he places it at the very end of his credo and describes it only briefly. With the exception of these short references Maimonides essentially ignores resurrection, concentrating instead on the immortality of the mind. Every human being, he argued, is composed of a body and soul, and the soul, particularly the intellect, is the "form" or "idea" of the body. In fact, he states: "The soul referred to in this connection is not the soul which is needed for the body but the form of the soul (*tzurat hanefesh*) which is the knowledge it derives from God" (*Mishneh Torah,* Repentance 8:3).

In a remarkable passage in *Guide to the Perplexed,* which deals with a similar issue (and where the idea of resurrection is conspicuously absent), Maimonides writes: "Soul (*nefesh*) . . . is also a term denoting the rational soul, I mean the form of man. . . . And it is a term denoting the thing that remains of man after death.[7]

Again, in a discussion of the world to come in his *Mishneh Torah,* Maimonides argues that

> In the World to Come, there is nothing corporeal, and no material substance; there are only souls of the righteous without bodies—like the ministering angels. . . . The righteous attain to a knowledge and realization of truth concerning God to which they had not attained while they were in the murky and lowly body.[8]

Maimonides' writings on the immortality of the intellect created such a stir among his contemporaries that he felt compelled to defend himself against those who accused him of not believing in the resurrection of the body.[9] He therefore wrote an essay entitled "Treatise on Resurrection," and in an attempt to explain his position to the general population, said:

> What may, in all likelihood, have led men to misjudge us is the fact that while we dilate on the dogma of immortality,

offering appropriate illustrations from scriptural and rabbinical authorities, we are, on the contrary, very brief when alluding to resurrection and content ourselves with the mere assertion that it is an essential creed of our religion. . . . It is faith and not reason that can persuade us that it [resurrection] will occur. . . . No proof can be advanced in support thereof. How then could it be expected that we should have discussed it at length?[10]

While Maimonides may have been reserved in elaborating his personal belief of resurrection, others were not. For example, Sheshet ben Isaac of Saragossa (1131–1209), a Maimonidean supporter, claimed that there is no resurrection other than the eternal life of the soul of the sage-philosopher. He ridiculed those who actually believed that the bodies will be revived in the future:

I ask this fool who maintains that the souls will return to the dead corpses and that they are destined to return to the soil of Israel: Into which body will the soul return? If it is to the body from which it has departed [then this will] already have returned to its elements thousands of years earlier. . . . If, however, this soul is to return to another body which God will create, then it is another man who will be created in his own time and has not been dead.[11]

After Maimonides' death, his views on the soul's immortality were forcefully defended by another great Jewish philosopher, Levi ben Gerson, usually called Gersonides (1288–1344). He, too, argued that the knowledge individuals acquired in life is indestructible. The totality of these accumulated ideas represents our only possible immortality.

We find a similar idea in the writings of the great Jewish philosopher Baruch Spinoza (1632–1677), for whom knowledge was the eternal part of every human being. According to Spinoza, the more knowledge we have the greater our participation in eternity. Spinoza, unlike Maimonides, wrote without ambiguity. He said what he meant. As a result, he was "put into *cherem*," excommunicated by the rabbinate, a ban that has not been revoked by the Orthodox to this day.

Immortality in Modern Thought

Many contemporary Orthodox Jews affirm the talmudic belief in immortality of the soul combined with resurrection of the body. Thus, one liturgical passage from the Orthodox prayer book reads:

> O my God, the soul which Thou gavest me is pure; Thou didst create it, Thou didst form it, Thou didst breathe into me. Thou preservest it within me, and Thou wilt take it from me, but wilt restore unto me hereafter. So long as the soul is within me, I will give thanks unto Thee, O Lord my God and God of my fathers, Sovereign of all works, Lord of all souls! Blessed art Thou, O Lord, who restorest souls unto the dead.[12]

Commenting on one section of this prayer—"restore [it] unto me" —the author, Joseph H. Hertz, writes, "Here the doctrine of the immortality of the soul is affirmed."[13] Yet from the text of the entire prayer, we know that immortality is only one component of the eternal life, the other being resurrection of the body, as seen from the phrases "restore unto me hereafter" and "who restorest souls unto the dead."

Immortality of the individual soul was embraced by many modern thinkers. The first major Jewish philosopher of the Enlightenment, Moses Mendelssohn, affirmed that the human soul is not only imperishable, but also possesses self-awareness. To assume the contrary, he added, would be incompatible with the idea of God's goodness and justice.

Most non-Orthodox Jews have by now deemphasized or rejected the belief in bodily resurrection and affirm instead the idea of the soul's immortality. Reform Jews, especially, have made this idea a major doctrine of their Judaism. Yet, as one scholar recently pointed out, by soul, the early Reform Jews did not mean the medieval sort of inner substance modern science has discredited. Instead they had recourse to nineteenth-century philosophy's emphasis on the human "spirit."[14] Similarly Mordecai Kaplan, the founder of the Jewish Reconstructionist movement, wrote: "The soul is nothing other than the human being as a person or self."[15]

An affirmation of immortality and a rejection of resurrection were included among the resolutions of the Philadelphia Conference of American Reform Rabbis (1869) then reaffirmed in the Pittsburgh Platform of 1885. Kaufmann Kohler, one of the conveners of the Pittsburgh Conference, based the idea of immortality "on the God-likeness of the human soul, which is the mirror of Divinity."[16] He added: "He who recognizes the unchangeable will of an all-wise, all-ruling God in the immutable laws of nature must find it impossible to praise God according to the traditional formula as the "reviver of the dead" but will avail himself instead of the expression used in the *Union Prayer Book* after the pattern of Einhorn: "He who has implanted within us immortal life."[17]

This last formulation was not a new invention but was taken from the traditional blessing after the reading of the Torah, when we say, "Blessed is the Lord our God, Ruler of the universe, who has given us a Torah of truth, implanting within us eternal life. Blessed is the Lord, Giver of the Torah."[18]

Gates of Prayer contains a number of passages alluding to the idea of immortality. The traditional prayer *Elohai Neshamah* appears in *Gates of Prayer* as follows:

> The soul that You have given me, O God, is a pure one! You have created and formed it, breathed it into me, and within me You sustain it. So long as I have breath, therefore, I will give thanks to You, O Lord my God and God of all ages, Master of all creation, Lord of every human spirit.
>
> Blessed is the Lord, in whose hands are the souls of all the living and the spirits of all flesh.   (p. 53)

During a memorial service, one reads:

> Only this have we been taught, and in this we put our trust: from You comes the spirit, and to You it must return.
>
>   (p. 548)

At a house of mourning, one prays:

> O Lord, God of the spirits of all flesh, You are close to the hearts of the sorrowing, to strengthen and console them with

the warmth of Your love, and with the assurance that the human spirit is enduring and indestructible. (p. 646)

Before the Kaddish, one of the meditations is entitled "The Spirit Lives On" (p. 627) and includes the statement "The dust returns to the earth, the spirit lives on with God" (cf. Eccles. 12:7).

In Summary

The idea of immortality has had a very powerful appeal among Jews. Whether it is the "soul," "intellect," or "spirit" that is eternal, many believers affirm that even after death something of us remains forever. It is this assurance that enables them to face life with greater courage and hope.

NOTES

1. D. A. Wells, *God, Man and the Thinker* (New York: Random House, 1964), pp. 192–93.
2. See Chapter Three above.
3. "On the Giants," Philo, *Complete Works*, Vol. 2, trans. F. H. Colson and G. H. Whitaker (London: W. Heinemann, and New York: G. P. Putnam's Sons, 1929), p. 451.
4. H. A. Wolfson, *Philo*, Vol. 1 (Cambridge, Mass.: Harvard University Press, 1962), p. 404.
5. Ibid., "The Posterity and Exile of Cain," p. 409.
6. Helek: *Sanhedrin*, Chap. 10; Twersky, *A Maimonides Reader*, p. 414.
7. Moses Maimonides, *Guide to the Perplexed*, 1:41, trans. S. Pines (Chicago: University of Chicago Press, 1963), p. 91.
8. Repentance 8, quoted in J. J. Minkin, *The World of Moses Maimonides* (New York: Thomas Yoseloff, 1957), p. 406.
9. See "Maimonidean Controversy," *Encyclopaedia Judaica* [hereafter referred to as *E.J.*], Vol. 11, pp. 745–54.
10. Quoted by Minkin, *The World of Moses Maimonides*, p. 403.
11. Quoted in *E.J.*, Vol. 11, p. 748.
12. Joseph H. Hertz, *The Authorized Daily Prayer Book* (New York: Bloch Publishing Co., 1975), p. 19.
13. Ibid., and notes.
14. E. B. Borowitz, *Liberal Judaism* (New York: UAHC, 1984), p. 214.
15. Mordecai Kaplan, *The Meaning of God in Modern Jewish Religion* (New York: Reconstructionist Press, 1962), p. 113.
16. Quoted in Plaut, *The Growth of Reform Judaism*, p. 215.
17. Ibid.
18. *Gates of Prayer*, p. 419.

·5·

Reincarnation

Basic Idea

The idea that a soul enters another living entity after the death of its body has intrigued people for centuries. Cultures both ancient and modern have made this notion a basic tenet of their religious ideology. It appears prominently in Hinduism, in the burial customs of many tribes in Africa, in ancient Greek philosophy, and in Judaism, primarily among mystics and in Chasidism.

In Hebrew the technical term for this idea is *gilgul neshamot*, literally "turning" or "rolling" of souls. In English three different terms are used: reincarnation, transmigration of souls, and metempsychosis (from the Greek, "to put a soul in or over").

We do not know how this idea entered Judaism. One finds no clear references to reincarnation in the Bible, though later mystics read many of their own ideas into the text. Similarly some Jewish commentators tried to find mention of reincarnation in the writings of the first-century Jewish historian Josephus and in talmudic texts. Anan ben David, the eighth-century founder of Karaism, a Jewish sect, reportedly believed in reincarnation. By the twelfth century, however, the idea of transmigration appears to be taken for granted in the Kabbalah, the Jewish mystical literature, and remains a Jewish option for belief today, with or without biblical "proof."

Preexistence of Souls

Those who embrace reincarnation hold that souls have an independent life, existing before and after the death of the body. The

46

soul, they say, joins the body at an appropriate time, remains with it for a specified period, then takes leave of the body about the time of death, ready to assume its next "assignment" in the physical world. The souls of human beings help determine the destination of their reincarnation.

The Zohar, the classic text of the early Kabbalah, states:

> It is the path taken by man in this world that determines the path of the soul on her departure. Thus, if a man is drawn towards the Holy One, and is filled with longing towards Him in this world, the soul in departing . . . is carried upward towards the higher realms by the impetus given her each day in this world.[1]

[Note how the "soul" (*neshamah,* a Hebrew feminine noun) is referred to as "she."]

The Kabbalists realized that not all righteous individuals in this world receive their due rewards. Some suffer, even though they observe the commandments of the Torah. Reincarnation seemed a plausible answer to this "injustice." Some Kabbalists argued that the pain a righteous person suffers in this world is not necessarily a result of personal sins but rather a consequence of acts committed in a previous incarnation. This notion was also offered as an explanation for the tragic death of infants. Their early demise, said the Kabbalists, was a result of sins committed by an ancestor in an earlier *gilgul.* It was, therefore, not the child who was being punished but rather the soul of the previous sinner.

Kabbalists also used reincarnation to explain odd or unusual occurrences of human characteristics. They asked, for example, why some individuals act like animals. The answer offered is that these people carry the soul of a beast.

Why do some females remain barren, unable to conceive a child? Because they are endowed with the soul that formerly resided in a man. Converts to Judaism were assumed to be individuals whose souls had previously inhabited a Jewish person.

Whereas some Kabbalists believed reincarnation applied exclusively to human beings, others held that it also included animals and even inanimate objects. In *The Dybbuk,* a popular play based on Jewish folklore, one of the characters says:

> The souls of the wicked return in the form of beasts, or birds or fish—or plants even—and are powerless to purify themselves by their own efforts. They have to wait for the coming of some righteous sage to purge them of their sins and set them free. Others enter the bodies of the newly born and cleanse themselves by well doing.[2]

Purpose of Reincarnation

In early kabbalistic writings, the perceived purpose for transmigration of souls was to inflict punishment for a variety of offenses. Thus, for example, we find in the Zohar: "Now the spirit which has left this world without procreation and engendering of children undergoes constant transmigration, finding no rest . . .[3]

In addition, early Kabbalism viewed reincarnation as an opportunity for the soul to cleanse itself of impurities before moving on. In time the view of transmigration evolved from that of a punishment for individual transgressions to that of a collective hereafter for all the souls of Israel—indeed, for all human beings. It became a vehicle for atonement.

In Jewish mystical thinking, reincarnation is not a substitute for resurrection, only a stage of the soul as it goes from one *gilgul* to another. The ultimate goal is still resurrection, a reunification of the body and soul and eternal life in the world to come. A particularly critical question for many people was: How many cycles of existence are required to purify my soul? Some Kabbalists state that in order for a righteous soul to atone, it needs to undergo three reincarnations, while the wicked soul may need as many as a thousand.

Gilgul, Ibbur, *and* Dybbuk

The Kabbalists describe three types of reincarnation: *gilgul, ibbur,* and *dybbuk. Gilgul* takes place during pregnancy. *Ibbur* (impregnation) occurs when an "old" soul enters the body of another individual at any time during its lifetime. The soul dwells in the new body for a limited period and performs certain acts or commandments. Finally, when an evil soul enters a person, causing mental illness and temporarily manifesting itself as a foreign personality, the invading soul is called *dybbuk*.[4]

The presence of a *dybbuk* in an individual is troublesome, both for the person and for the evil spirit that has invaded the body. In order to give respite to both, the *dybbuk* must be exorcised. Kabbalistic literature is full of stories of such exorcisms and even describes procedures for this purpose in great detail. The power to perform exorcisms was attributed solely to well-known sages called *baalei-shem* (master of the Name [of God]). Israel ben Eliezer (1700–1760), also known as the Baal Shem Tov, the founder of the Chasidic movement in Eastern Europe, was such an exorcist.

S. Ansky's play, *The Dybbuk*, which we have already mentioned, describes a remarkable exorcism. Leah, a young bride, is possessed by a *dybbuk*, which is the soul of her predestined groom. Her father has previously arranged for a friend's son to marry Leah, but the young man dies. As Leah's wedding ceremony is about to commence, the soul of the dead young man enters Leah and possesses her.

A prominent rabbi is called to exorcise the *dybbuk* but fails. Finally another rabbi comes in, asks that all present dress up in shrouds, that black candles be lit, and that the altar in the sanctuary be covered with black curtains. Once this is done, he addresses the *dybbuk* in front of the entire congregation:

> Sinful and obstinate soul, with the power of Almighty God, and with the sanction of the Holy Scriptures, I, Azrael ben Hadassah, do with these words send asunder every cord that binds you to the world of living creatures, and to the body and soul of the maiden Leah, daughter of Channah . . . and do pronounce you excommunicated from all Israel.[5]

The rabbi directs that the shofar (ram's horn) be blown, after which the *dybbuk* finally leaves the body.

In kabbalistic or chasidic literature, many mental illnesses are interpreted as invasions by *dybbukim.* People with emotional problems assume they are possessed by evil or good spirits. Some maintain they carry the souls of important historical figures. King David is considered the reincarnation of Adam, and Job the reincarnation of Abraham's father, Terah. As late as 1903, some Jews in Baghdad underwent a ceremony of exorcism believing they carried the soul of the false messiah Shabbetai Zvi (seventeenth century). According to Gershom Scholem, "The phenomena connected with the beliefs in and the stories about *dybbukim* usually have their factual background in cases of hysteria and sometimes even in manifestations of schizophrenia."[6]

Proponents and Opponents

The idea of reincarnation has been both defended and attacked with great fervor over the centuries. During the Middle Ages, one of the great Kabbalists, Rabbi Menassah ben Israel (1604–1657), claimed:

> The belief in the doctrine of the transmigration of souls is a firm and infallible dogma accepted by the whole assemblage of our Church with one accord, so that there is none to be found who would dare deny it.[7]

Another medieval Jewish philosopher, Abraham bar Hiyya of Spain (who lived during the first half of the twelfth century), taught that if a person is ignorant but righteous, his soul returns once or twice more, attaching itself to bodies, until it obtains knowledge and wisdom.

Most of the nonmystical Jewish philosophers in the Middle Ages, however, rejected the doctrine. Some of them, including Judah Halevi and Maimonides, totally ignored it. Saadia ben Yosef al-Fayyumi (892–942) argued that the soul and the body constitute one unit and that a human body cannot unite with an animal soul or vice versa. Abraham ibn Daud (born 1110) maintained that the soul of a person is matched exclusively to its body. One cannot have the soul of another unless the two bodies are identical.

Joseph Albo (1340–1444) raised a number of questions regarding reincarnation:

> Why should a soul which has already functioned in a human body and has become a free agent return to the body again? And why should the seminal drop [of man that creates the body] have the capacity to receive a soul which has already functioned in a body rather than to receive a soul which has not functioned in a body and is not a free agent? . . . God knows.[8]

Modern Ideas

In modern times, mystics still defend the idea of reincarnation. Many chasidic leaders who follow the teachings of the Kabbalah promote it as a basic Jewish belief.

Moses Teitelbaum (1759–1841), an important representative of the Hungarian Chasidim, commenting on the biblical verse "He took curds . . . and the calf that had been prepared" (Gen. 18:8), writes:

> My master and holy *tzadik* Jacob Isaac of Lublin, of blessed memory, once asked me, Why is there no mention of fish in the holy Torah when it relates the story of the angels and their meal? Yet the rabbis generally speak of meat and fish when referring to a meal. I replied that the main purpose of eating meals is in order to elevate the holy sparks in the food and to put right the souls of those who have been reincarnated. In the writings of the Ari [i.e., Isaac Luria (1534–1572), the great Kabbalist of Safed], of blessed memory, it is said that the majority of *tzadikim* come back to earth as fish. It is certain that this only applies to *tzadikim* of lesser rank, but great *tzadikim* do not need to come back to earth again for further perfection.[9]

Teitelbaum takes reincarnation for granted, assuming that a person's soul comes to earth in order "to put right" the sins he or she had committed in a previous existence. Therefore, when a *tzadik* eats and digests fish, he or she helps perfect the reincarnated soul of a previous *tzadik*.

Proponents of Kabbalah continue to defend the belief in reincarnation today. For example, Philip S. Berg, an ordained Orthodox rabbi and the dean of the Research Centre of Kabbalah International, argues that "Reincarnation is not a question of faith or doctrine, but of logic and reason."[10] He maintains that transmigration is a key that unlocks many mysteries:

> Is there no law or purpose in the assignment of the law in our respective destinies? One man may work hard all his life and at the very end of it wind up an in-patient in a dreary hospital or charity home. Another inherits a vast estate and draws upon the luxuries of the world as though they were his personal bank account, even though he may be an idler, a parasite, a useless member of society. Why should this be so? . . . What we need today is a master key to unlock the apparent chaos and find order within it. Reincarnation, stripped of superstition and half-truth, can be that key.[11]

In Berg's opinion, reincarnation serves a very special purpose. Our bodies, he argues, are accustomed to receiving. The soul, on the other hand, has a higher goal.

> Learning to share, with rejection of greed that says, take it all, thus becomes the soul's mission in life—and in life after life, depends upon the soul's progress toward that goal.[12]

The teachings about reincarnation are not reserved for the elite, but open to the average individual. In 1986, Rabbi Gedaliah Fleer of Jerusalem visited Boston for a number of workshops on Kabbalah and mysticism. *The Jewish Advocate,* a newspaper in Boston, reported:

> Like Eastern religions, Judaism believes in reincarnation. "It has many aspects," Rabbi Fleer said, citing *gilgul*—a concept similar to karma in that it involves repayment for actions in

past lives—and *ibbur,* in which "the sparks of the soul of someone deceased join the soul of someone living in order to strengthen that person in ways he couldn't come to on his own."

"It is not the whole soul but certain sparks which are reincarnated," Fleer asserted. "Every time a soul is born it is perfected . . . [by] the limitations of the conditions into which we are born. The aspect that has become more perfect is not reborn. . . . The parts that remain undeveloped, which have never been actualized or brought to fruition," which Fleer associates with the subconscious, "that's what comes back."

This concept of reincarnation, that a spark from one soul can be born into another person, is, according to Rabbi Fleer, the deeper meaning of the idea that "every Jew is responsible for every other Jew."[13]

In Summary

Outside of the circle dedicated to Kabbalah and mysticism, a belief in reincarnation is not widespread among Jews today, though it has a powerful appeal. There is no doubt that it provides one answer to the perplexing question of divine justice in the world and a hope for life after death. But is it true? Can it happen? Does it occur? Only those who believe in reincarnation can answer with conviction.

NOTES

1. H. Sperling and M. Simon, trans. *The Zohar,* II, 99b (London: Soncino I), p. 324.
2. S. Ansky (pseud. Solomon Rapaport (1863–1920), *The Dybbuk,* trans. G. Alsberg and Winifred Katzin (New York: Horace Liveright, 1926), pp. 81ff.
3. *Zohar,* II, 99b; Soncino III, pp. 302–303.
4. Gershom Scholem, the great scholar of Jewish mysticism, considers *dybbuk* an abbreviated form of the words *dybbuk meruach raah* (a cleavage of an evil spirit), or *dybbuk min hachitzonim* (dybbuk from the demonic side). See his *Kabbalah* (New York: Meridian, 1978), p. 349.
5. Ansky, *Dybbuk,* pp. 135–36.
6. Scholem, *Kabbalah,* p. 350.
7. J. Head and S. L. Cranston, eds., *Reincarnation: An East-West Anthology* (New York: The Julian Press, 1961), p. 29.
8. Joseph Albo, *Book of Principles,* Vol. 4, trans. I. Husik (Philadelphia: JPS, 1946), pp. 287–88.

9. Louis Jacobs, *Hasidic Thought* (New York: Behrman House, 1976), p. 179.

10. Philip S. Berg, *The Wheels of a Soul* (Jerusalem; New York: Research Centre of Kabbalah, 1984), p. 29.

11. Ibid., p. 26.

12. Ibid., p. 83.

13. Judith Antonelli "Jerusalem Rabbi's Magical Mystical Tour," *The Jewish Advocate,* November 27, 1986, 6.

·6·

Living on through Deeds

Death Is Not the End

In discussing the question of "immortality in Judaism," Rabbi Israel Mattuck observed: "All belief in salvation implies a valuation."[1] Judaism lacks a dogmatic theology. Thus, every statement about afterlife reflects values we cherish most. Though many Jewish thinkers have definite ideas regarding a life after death, others attempt to define immortality within the natural realm.

In support of the idea of immortality, Rabbi J. Leonard Levy (1865–1917) argued:

> We know that everything that has once been brought into existence cannot be put out of existence. The word I now speak is spoken forever; it can never be recalled. The soul once propelled into the universe cannot be put out of it; it can never be destroyed. What becomes of it after death I know not.[2]

Other Jewish thinkers of our time have argued that though our physical life comes to an end, we keep on living mostly by virtue of certain deeds we carry out as human beings. We must look for our immortality, they aver, not among the fanciful ideas of resurrection, or reincarnation, or even in the everlasting life of our souls (whatever that means) but in the work we have accomplished in this world, work that has a lasting value.

Different Ideas

In his classic *Basic Judaism*, Rabbi Milton Steinberg wrote:

Death cannot be and is not the end of life. Man transcends death in many altogether naturalistic fashions. He may be immortal biologically, through his children; in thought, through the survival of his memory; in influence, by virtue of the continuance of his personality as a force among those who come after him; and ideally, through his identification with the timeless things of the spirit.[3]

Similarly, Rabbi Roland B. Gittelsohn maintained that after death we live through nature, through our children, through our group, and in the good we do.[4]

In a published sermon entitled "A Jewish View of Immortality," Rabbi Bernard S. Raskas wrote:

What is this immortality in which I believe?
I believe that a person lives on in his or her family. . . .
I believe there is a form of immortality in the institutions we
build and the causes we espouse. . . .
I believe in the immortality of friendship and helpfulness. . . .
I believe in the immortality of existence. . . .
I find immortality in my people. . . .[5]

These Jewish thinkers have affirmed that Judaism emphasizes deed over creed, practice over theological speculation. Three modern views of immortality result from this thinking:

1. Biological immortality
2. Immortality through influence
3. Immortality through deeds.

Biological Immortality

The idea that we share in the immortality of humanity is uplifting. Rabbi Joshua Loth Liebman wrote: "As we link ourselves to all of the heroes and sages and martyrs, to all of the poets and thinkers of every race and every clime, we become part of a great and moving drama."[6]

Not all of us are poets or thinkers, but we can identify with the "wisest thoughts, the noblest ideals, the richest music of the centuries."[7]

After death we still live through nature, as Gittelsohn pointed out:

> Our bodies no longer live after death, but they are then transformed into other kinds of life. The energy and chemical elements from our bodies go into the soil, where they help make flowers grow and directly or indirectly provide food for plants, animals, and human beings. Thus, we, who come from nature, return to nature.[8]

Rabbi Raskas quotes Harry Emerson Fosdick, who wrote:

> We ask the leaf, "Are you complete in yourself?" And the leaf answers, "No, my life is in the trunk and branches and the leaf." So it is in the great tree of being. Everything is a part of all of existence.[9]

More concretely our immortality is achieved through our children and our children's children. We see in them a reflection of our personality. They carry our name, often bear our physical resemblance, and hold memories about us.

Ben Sira, the Jewish sage who lived in Jerusalem around the second century B.C.E., wrote: "Call no one happy before his death; a man will be known through his children" (11:28, RSV). Also: "The father may die, and yet he is not dead, for he has left behind him one like himself" (30:4, RSV).

Not only do we live on through the lives of our children but by identifying with our social group, we share in its immortality. Raskas writes:

> I was with my people when they were part of the exodus from Egypt. I stood with them at Mount Sinai to receive the Ten Commandments. The pronouncements of Isaiah pound in my blood. The sayings of Akiba are sealed in the cells of my brain. The message of Maimonides is part of my mind. I experienced the Holocaust and shared in the agony of my people. I partici-

pated in the birth of modern Israel and the ecstasy of my people. I am a Jew, a corporate part of my people. I say this, not in arrogance, but in awesome humility. As a member of the Jewish people, I am immortal.[10]

Immortality through Influence

All of us have been influenced by parents, teachers, friends. In turn, we influence others, often even without knowing. We fashion ourselves after our teachers, our models, always remembering them. They live on in us.

Raskas writes:

> Every time I see a black achieve something, I think of Martin Luther King. Every time I touch down at the airport in Israel, I think of Theodor Herzl, David Ben-Gurion, and Golda Meir."[11]

In turn, we, too, influence others. We become models for those who look up to us. We fashion their lives. Liebman writes:

> We may not be sculptors, able to hew immortal statues out of immobile rock. Most of us, however, have the infinitely greater privilege (which we take too much for granted) of molding the spiritual life and destiny of the generations that come after us. Men and women whom we influence by the example of our lives, the children who are touched by the flame of our spirits—it is in them that we live on and find the flame of our eternal significance.[12]

There is a difference, however, between the biological and spiritual immortality we achieve through our children. As Gittelsohn indicates:

> In the former, it is automatic; the very act of procreation insures that we shall survive our own death physically. Our spiritual endurance beyond death, however, is dependent upon what our children do. If they condemn or scorn our values, there is no spiritual immortality through them.[13]

Immortality through Deeds

Our work can outlast our lives. Mozart died long ago, but his music is still with us. The writings of Maimonides, who lived in the Middle Ages, are studied diligently today. Herzl's Zionist dream lives in the form of the Jewish State of Israel. Who does not admire the writings of Shakespeare or the paintings of Chagall, the accomplishments of Einstein, the courage of Anne Frank? All of them will continue to live through their work. The rabbis of old knew this lesson well. They taught: "When a person dies, neither silver, nor gold, nor gems, nor pearls accompany him, but only [knowledge] of Torah and good deeds" (*Avot* 6:9).

Similarly we find written: "We need not erect monuments to the righteous; their deeds are their monuments" (*Gen. Rabbah* 32:10).

Rabbi Sidney Greenberg quotes a talmudic story to stress the point:

> A hungry fox was eyeing some luscious fruit in a garden, but to his dismay he could find no way to enter. At last he discovered an opening through which, he thought, he might possibly get in, but he soon found that the hole was too small to admit his body. "Well," he thought, "if I fast three days I will be able to squeeze through." He did so; and he now feasted to his heart's delight on the grapes and all the other good things in the orchard. But lo! when he wanted to escape before the owner of the garden would find him, he discovered to his great distress that the opening had again become too small for him. Poor animal! Again he had to fast three days, and as he escaped, he cast a farewell glance upon the scene of his late revels saying: "O garden, charming art thou, delicious are thy fruits! But what have I now for all my labor and cunning?"
>
> So it is with man. Naked he comes into the world; naked must he leave it. After all his toil therein he carries nothing away with him except the good deeds he leaves behind.[14]

Not everyone, however, has a creative mind or talented hand to leave behind a valuable piece of art. Most people live ordinary lives devoid of heroism and artistry. Though their works will not long endure, they, too, will live on through their children—more importantly, through the goodness they instilled in the hearts of others. They have become a "link" in the chain of humanity, a tie that binds one generation to another.

What of those who brought evil into the world? Do they become immortal?

The memory of Hitler will remain forever a blot on humanity. The biblical Haman, symbolizing the oppressor par excellence, lives forever cursed for his deeds. Similarly the murderer and the rapist will be remembered as shameful figures to be condemned, for they have impaired the progress of society. As Rabbi Gittelsohn points out, "The only immortality worthy of the name is that achieved by propelling evolution forward, not by holding it back."[15]

We can help prolong the influence of our forebears through the actions we take to perpetuate their memory. As their emissaries, we keep their dreams alive.

Rabbi Jacob J. Weinstein once wrote:

> We, the living, can determine the kind of immortality our beloved shall have. . . . We can act as their personal representatives to the living. Where they lifted the burden or worry from a fellow man, we can give encouragement and help; where they brought cheer and care and loyalty, we can be instead.[16]

A similar sentiment is expressed during a funeral service: "May the memory of our departed dear one inspire us with a stronger sense of duty and responsibility."[17]

In a prayer entitled "We Live in Our Work," we read:

> May the nobility in their lives and the high ideals they cherished endure in our thoughts and live on in our deeds. May we, carrying on their work, help to redeem Your promise that life shall prevail.[18]

Another prayer, "The Blessing of Memory," contains the statement "Those who live no more echo still within our thoughts and words, and what they did is part of what we have become."[19]

Ultimately we know that "death cannot kill what never dies" (William Penn), and a good name remains forever. The poet Hugh Robert Orr said it well:

> They are not dead who live
> in hearts they leave behind.
> In those whom they have blessed
> They live a life again,
> And shall live through the years
> Eternal life, and grow
> Each day more beautiful
> As time declares their good,
> Forgets the rest, and proves
> Their immortality.[20]

In Summary

Rejecting the traditional views of immortality through resurrection or reincarnation, some Jewish thinkers take a naturalistic view that eternal life occurs biologically through the children we bring into the world, through the influence we exert on others during our lives, or through the works we create that impact on our contemporaries and descendants—with memories of past deeds that either diminish or elevate the human spirit.

NOTES

1. Israel Mattuck, "Immortality in Judaism." Pamphlet by the Commission on Information About Education. (New York: UAHC, undated), p. 7.

2. J. Leonard Levy, *Prophetic Voice* (Pittsburgh, Pa.: Rodef Shalom Congregation, 1970), p. 86.

3. Milton Steinberg, *Basic Judaism* (New York: Harcourt, Brace and World, 1947), p. 160.

4. Gittelsohn, *Wings*, pp. 354–62.

5. Bernard S. Raskas, "A Jewish View of Immortality," *The American Rabbi,* 19/1 (August 1986), pp. 57–59.

6. Liebman, *Peace of Mind,* pp. 109–10.

7. Ibid.

8. Gittelsohn, *Wings*, p. 355.

9. Raskas, "A Jewish View of Immortality," p. 59.

10. Ibid.

11. Ibid, p. 58.
12. Liebman, *Peace of Mind,* p. 110.
13. Gittelsohn, *Wings,* pp. 357–58.
14. Sidney Greenberg, *A Treasury of Comfort* (Hollywood, Calif.: Wilshire Book Company, 1967), pp. 193–94.
15. Gittelsohn, *Wings,* p. 361.
16. Greenberg, *A Treasury of Comfort,* p. 225.
17. *Rabbi's Manual* (New York: CCAR, 1961), p. 87.
18. *Gates of Prayer,* p. 626.
19. Ibid., p. 625.
20. Greenberg, *A Treasury of Comfort,* pp. 23–24.

BIBLIOGRAPHY

(This Bibliography includes studies relevant to the first six chapters of this book.)

Ahad Ha-Am. *Selected Essays of Ahad Ha-Am.* New York: Meridian, 1962.

Albo, Joseph. *Book of Principles.* Translated by I. Husik, 4 vols. Philadelphia: JPS, 1946.

Ansky, S. *The Dybbuk.* Translated by H. G. Alsberg and W. Katzin. New York: Horace Liveright, 1926.

Antonelli, Judith. "Jerusalem Rabbi's Magical Mystical Tour," *The Jewish Advocate,* 27 November 1986, p. 6.

Berg, Philip S. *The Wheels of a Soul.* Jerusalem; New York: Research Centre of Kabbalah, 1984.

Borowitz, E. B. *Liberal Judaism.* New York: UAHC, 1984.

Eisenstein, I., ed. *Varieties of Jewish Belief.* New York: Reconstructionist Press, 1966.

Freud, Sigmund. *The Future of an Illusion.* New York: Anchor Press, 1964.

Gates of Prayer. New York: CCAR, 1975.

Gates of Repentance. New York: CCAR, 1978.

Gittelsohn, Roland B. *Wings of the Morning.* New York: UAHC, 1969.

Greenberg, Sidney. *A Treasury of Comfort.* Hollywood, Calif.: Wilshire Book Co., 1967.

Head, J., and Cranston, S.L., eds. *Reincarnation, an East-West Anthology.* New York: The Julian Press, 1961.

Herberg, Will. *Judaism and Modern Man.* New York: Harper and Row, 1965.

Hertz, Joseph H. *The Authorized Daily Prayer Book.* New York: Bloch, 1975.

Immanuel ben Solomon of Rome. *Tophet and Eden* (Hell and Paradise). Translated by Hermann Gollancz. London: University of London, 1921.

The Interpreter's Dictionary of the Bible, 4 vols. New York; Nashville, Tenn.: Abingdon Press, 1962.

Jacobs, Louis. *Hasidic Thought.* New York: Behrman, 1976.

———. *A Jewish Theology.* New York: Behrman, 1973.

Josephus, Flavius. *Complete Works.* Translated by W. Whiston. Grand Rapids, Mich.: Kregel, 1963.

Kaplan, Mordecai. *The Meaning of God in Modern Jewish Religion.* New York: Reconstructionist Press, 1962.

Lamm, Maurice. *The Jewish Way in Death and Mourning.* New York: Jonathan David, 1969.

Lang, Bernhard. "Afterlife—Ancient Israel's Changing Vision of the World Beyond," *Bible Review,* February 1988, 12–23.

Levy, J. Leonard. *Prophetic Voice.* Pittsburgh, Pa.: Rodef Shalom Congregation, 1970.

Levy, Richard. "Upon Arising: An Affirmation of Techiyat Hameitim," *Journal of Reform Judaism,* CCAR, Fall 1982, 12–20.

Liebman, Joshua L. *Peace of Mind*. New York: Bantam, 1961.

Maimonides, Moses. *Guide to the Perplexed*. Translated by S. Pines. Chicago: University of Chicago Press, 1963.

Mattuck, Israel. "Immortality in Judaism." Pamphlet by the Commission on Information About Education. New York: UAHC, undated, p. 7.

Minkin, J. J. *The World of Moses Maimonides*. New York: Thomas Yoseloff, 1957.

Montefiore, C. G., and Loewe, H., eds. *A Rabbinic Anthology*. Cleveland, Ohio; New York: Meridian Books, 1963.

Moore, J. F. *Judaism*. Cambridge, Mass.: Harvard University Press, 1962.

The New Oxford Annotated Bible. Revised Standard Version. New York: Oxford University Press, 1973.

Philo of Alexandria. *Complete Works*. Translated by F. H. Colson and G. H. Whitaker. The Loeb Classical Library. London: W. Heinemann, and New York: G. P. Putnam, 1929.

Plaut, W. Gunther. *The Growth of Reform Judaism*. New York: WUPJ, 1965.

———. *The Rise of Reform Judaism*. New York: WUPJ, 1963.

Pritchard, James B.,ed. *Ancient Near Eastern Texts Relating to the Old Testament* [ANET]. Princeton, N.J.: Princeton University Press, 1969.

Rabbi's Manual. New York: CCAR, 1961, 1988.

Raskas, Bernard S., "A Jewish View of Immortality," *The American Rabbi*, 19/1, August 1986, 57–59.

Ringgren, Helmer. *Israelite Religion*. Philadelphia: Fortress Press, 1966.

Rubenstein, Richard L. "The Making of a Rabbi." In *Varieties of Jewish Belief*, edited by I. Eisenstein. New York: Reconstructionist Press, 1966.

Saadia ben Yosef al-Fayyumi. *The Book of Beliefs and Opinions*. Translated by Samuel Rosenblatt. New Haven, Conn.: Yale University Press, 1948.

Scholem, Gershom. *Kabbalah*. New York: Meridian, 1978.

The Soncino Talmud, 18 vols. London; New York: Soncino, 1935.

Sperling H., and Simon, M., trans. *The Zohar*, 5 vols. London: Soncino, 1956.

Steinberg, Milton. *Basic Judaism*. New York: Harcourt, Brace and World, 1947.

Tanach, A New Translation of the Holy Scriptures According to the Traditional Hebrew Text. Philadelphia: JPS, 1985.

Twersky, Isadore. *A Maimonides Reader*. New York: Behrman House, 1972.

Union Prayer Book, 2 vols. New York: CCAR, 1940 (Vol. I), 1945 (Vol. II).

Wolfson, H. A. *Philo*, 2 vols. Cambridge, Mass.: Harvard University Press, 1962.

Part II

CONTEMPORARY THINKERS

Introduction to Part Two

The classic Jewish positions presented in prior chapters constitute an overview of the historical spectrum of Jewish ideas regarding the afterlife. The chapters that follow contain deeply held personal views of prominent contemporary Jewish thinkers.

The six men and women you are about to meet were asked to reflect upon their own immortality. We hope their reactions, emerging from Reform, Conservative, and Orthodox backgrounds, will serve to illustrate the profound and moving manner in which Jewish theoretical positions have found expression in actual lives.

· 7 ·

Here and Hereafter

RABBI ALEXANDER M. SCHINDLER

Rabbi Alexander M. Schindler was born in Munich, Germany, in 1925. His father, Eliezer, was a Yiddish poet, his mother, Sali, a prominent businesswoman.

From an early age, young Alex was taught by his father to love everything Jewish. The family home was a traditional one, and he attended an Orthodox day school. But he also was a frequent worshiper at the great Reform Congregation in Munich. His chasidic grandparents touched his life, as did his mother's liberal professional friends. His family tree included a *sofer* of the Baal Shem Tov in Galicia and a radical classical Reform rabbi from Boston, and Alex was imbued with a respect for the rich tapestry of Jewish life.

The Schindler family came to the United States during the 1930s. Alex entered college at the age of fifteen, intending to become an engineer, but, after serving in the U.S. Army Ski Troops during World War II, the course of his life changed. The atrocities of the Nazi Holocaust and his father's influence led him to a passionate interest in Jewish history and Jewish life.

Ultimately he entered rabbinical school and was ordained from the Hebrew Union College-Jewish Institute of Religion in 1953. He served as a congregational rabbi in Worcester, Massachusetts, then joined the staff of the Union of American Hebrew Congregations, first as the director of the New England Council and subsequently as national director of Education. In 1973 he was elected president of the UAHC. Shortly thereafter he was also elected chairman of the Conference of Presidents of Major American Jewish Organizations.

Today, in his continuing leadership of the Reform movement, Rabbi Schindler is considered one of the foremost spokespeople for world Jewry.

When Dan Syme and Rifat Sonsino asked me to contribute to their volume on immortality, I instinctively demurred. After all, I am neither scholar nor theologian but activist, concerned essentially with the here and now.

On further reflection I acceded to their request. Having experienced death about me, I certainly have bent my mind to bear upon what happens beyond it. And, as a rabbi, it is my office to share my inmost thoughts with others.

Moreover, I have come to the conclusion that immanence and transcendence are inextricably intertwined. Seeking one, we find the other, too. When we Jews pray, when we praise God, when we recite blessings over the proceedings of our daily lives, what are we doing but affirming and experiencing the holiness of the so-called commonplace. What are we doing but focusing our attention on the here and now, so that we may experience the world's transcendent, loving nature.

This has been my own experience: the closer I feel to life at each lived moment, the closer I feel to God. Likewise, the closer I feel to God, the more involved and loving I feel to the life that surrounds me. From such feelings of "closeness" have emerged my most powerful and transformative experiences—including my ever-increasing confidence in the existence of a life after death for our souls.

To put the matter differently and, perhaps, more to the point, the closer I feel to the "here," the more confident I feel about the reality of the "hereafter."

The philosopher George Santayana came nearest to limning my own belief in immortality when he alluded to it as the soul's "invincible surmise." The phrase is wonderfully curious, for how can a "surmise," a belief that lacks evidence, boast of "invincibility"?

I believe I understand Santayana's wordplay, now, beyond my sixtieth year of life, when I have undergone most of my major life passages—as a soldier, husband, father, rabbi—and having felt the joys of life and the presence of the angel of death many, many times. Truly it is the least tangible forces of life that I now cherish as most real and most dear: love, hope, ideas, ideals. These "surmises" of my soul, rather than tangible honors or scars, make me who I am; these "surmises" of my soul prepare me for the final life passage by shielding me from fear.

In my case, the "surmise" of life hereafter took these many years and many life passages to gain its force of "invincibility."

As a youth, I was rather cavalier about the matter. Death is natural, I thought to myself, without depth or inspiration—if I thought about it at all. Like most young people, I was too busy seeing my place in the world to concern myself with vacating that place; I was too embroiled in constructing the future to perceive immortality near at hand.

Oddly enough my unconcern about life after death persisted even through my army years, although I served during World War II in three European campaigns and became altogether accustomed to the sight of lifeless bodies. Perhaps that was the reason for my incuriosity on the subject: wars cheapen life and devalue the loss of it. Perhaps, too, the energy required for sheer physical and mental survival could not be sustained were I even to have contemplated that my life could come to an end; I therefore sought solace not in thoughts of life after death but in memories of life before war and hopes for my personal, living future.

Perhaps, too, the feelings of belonging and of a larger purpose that fuel our faith in the afterlife were very much satisfied in me by the larger cause of extirpating the evil of Nazism from this earth. We were, after all, engaged in a genuinely global conflict with the fate of the human race in the balance. World War II is thus remembered by many men of my generation as the one time in their lives when they experienced a transformative meaning and a purpose for their sacrificial endeavors.

My years of rabbinic study following the war also failed to awaken my concern for the subject of the hereafter. To be sure, it was an element in my studies—in Bible, theology, Jewish philosophy—but it remained an intellectual exercise that never came to touch the depth of my being. If anything, *disbelief* was stirred in those years by the contrariety of views presented by our tradition:

*   *   *

The Bible conceives of life after death as a return of the body and soul to nature. The Talmud—so our teachers instructed us—offers some reflections on the immortality of the disembodied soul but fails to develop these ideas with any fullness.

Maimonides (RamBam) speaks with greater certitude of a lasting life for souls—but only for the bodiless souls of the righteous, while the souls of the wicked are doomed to perdition. Deathlessness, to the RaMBaM, is not a quality inherent in the soul: it is the reward bestowed for a life of goodness.

Only Moses Mendelssohn held that *all* human souls, each individually, are indestructible and deathless. But the neo-Kantian, Hermann Cohen, quickly refuted him, denying the possibility of the individual soul's survival. Cohen held forth only the promise that individuals survive in the "historic continuity of the people." Most modern Jewish philosophers hold with Cohen—and the circle back to the biblical concept of immortality as a "return to nature" is almost complete. . . .

What possible comfort would I find in these disputations, I asked myself, when as rabbi I would have to hold the hands of the dying and the bereaved? What consolation was there in these Jewish speculations for a student who had just completed an undergraduate honors thesis on the evolution of the Nazi war against the Jews? I had just finished reading fifty volumes of documents presented at the Nuremberg trials; I had just chastened my soul with an exhausting contemplation of the depths to which human beings can descend. I found no comfort whatsoever in the thought that the six million live on in some nebulous manner through the rest of the Jewish people and the rest of humankind.

"Remember thy last end and cease from enmity." In contemplating the significance of death, I could go no further than these words from the Apocrypha. I simply said to myself: We can't possibly know anything about the other side of death. Let's stick with one world at a time and conduct ourselves in *this* world in such a way that if there is an afterlife with God, we will be worthy of it.

So does the psalmist of the 88th Psalm question: "Do You work wonders for the dead?/ Do the shades rise to praise You?/Is Your faithful care recounted in the grave,/ Your constancy in the place of perdition?/ Are Your wonders made known in the netherworld,/ Your beneficient deeds in the land of oblivion?/ As for me, I cry out to You, O Lord; each morning my prayer greets You."

Perhaps in my agnosticism about the afterlife I was being altogether faithful to Judaism.

The death of my beloved father in 1957, in conjunction with my work as a rabbi in homes made sad and still by death, marked an awakening for me to the intuition that death was a portal rather than a sealed wall. The fullness of life—of family, professions, and fatherhood—was ripe on my vines; my sense of love for human beings, of belonging to the human race, were greatly heightened by sharing these most basic yet most meaningful life experiences. I found the idea that all this fullness would end in oblivion to be utterly mad. How could it be thus that all that animates life—the capacity to know, to create, to love, to dream—could be snuffed out like a sputtering candle, leaving not even a shadow? Too many of life's own ways—the reawakening of spring after deathlike winter, the miracle of birth from the inner space of our bodies, the constant transformation and exchange of all matter and energy, the notion of a "curved" universe—all testified against the likelihood that death could mean obliteration rather than transformation. Thus it was that my "surmise" began to attain its "invincible" force.

Many men and women whom I encountered shared and reinforced that faith. They were every bit as modern and as "enlightened" as I saw myself to be. There was Jimmy Heller, for instance. He was the rabbi of one of the largest Reform congregations in our land, a well-educated, brilliant Renaissance man. He was a leader of Labor Zionism. He wrote the program notes for the Cincinnati symphony. He was a ranking bridge player. His writings and preachings were soulful and intellectually powerful. And he believed with full faith in immortality, in the deathlessness of the soul—of each individual soul, with a full awareness of its particular past and being. Heller held these beliefs even when he was young and strong and articulated them forcefully in an extensive correspondence on the subject with Maurice Samuel.

I remember visiting Rabbi Heller on his deathbed. He was radiant with confidence. He did not regret his imminent passing. He saw it as precisely that, a "passing" from this world to another—to a world where he could once again embrace his father, and where he could enter into disputation—perhaps on the subject of immortality?—with Hermann Cohen and Moses Maimonides. I left his bedside with a sense that I would miss him rather than mourn him; I would feel his absence as one feels the absence of a traveler.

My own faith in the hereafter has never been the profoundly held conviction, the triumphant cry of faith, that was Jimmy Heller's. Yet there are aspects of immortality of which I have always been able to speak with assurance.

We certainly live on in the *memory* of those who knew us, loved us, and were influenced by our lives. My father died more than thirty years ago, yet to this day I think of him on almost a daily basis. Many of my ideas are stimulated by his specific thoughts and by his manner of thought—the ethical assumptions and creative processes that informed his intellectual life. Often I make my decisions by the measure of what my father would have wanted me to do. And whenever I think of him, the sense of his continued presence is stronger than the knowledge of his death.

We can also speak with assurance of the *immortality of the human deed*. The Talmud teaches that "we live in deeds, not years"; *Pirke Avot* affirms that "this world is like a vestibule before the world to come," yet declares in that same passage: "Better is one hour of repentance and good deeds in this world than the whole life in the world to come." Indeed, the contemplation of death can enable us to evaluate and purify our deeds: "All things which seem foolish in the light of death," said the nineteenth-century thinker and leader Claude G. Montefiore, "are really foolish in themselves." But those efforts that do retain their integrity in the face of death's finality are the very efforts that postpone finality again and again, for just as our bones nourish the earth, our deeds nourish the future.

When Chananiah ben Teradion, noblest of Jewish martyrs, was burned at the stake wrapped in a Scroll of the Law, his pupils who witnessed his terrible agony cried out: "Our master, our teacher, what seest thou?" And he replied: "I see the parchment burning—but the *letters* of the Law, they soar on high." Even so it is with us. Our flesh will decay, our fingers will crumble into dust, but what they create—in beauty and goodness and love— lives on for all time to come.

Thus do our deeds bridge that fearsome chasm that separates the world of life from the world of death; thus does the work of our hands endure. Thus do we will immortality for the human race; thus do we answer the calling of our genes.

The perspectives and conclusions of scientific inquiry are generally viewed as antithetical to the "invincible surmise." For me, however, these conclusions are bracing, not destructive, to my faith. The notion of the relativity of time, the reality of genetic inheritance, the ever-expanding sense of ecology and the interconnection of all things, mathematical flirtations with multidimensional worlds, the quantum notion of a nonmechanistic universe—these are all complex scientific concepts of which I have but a person's under- standing, yet they speak to me as metaphors that reinforce the potential of life hereafter.

Now, to be sure, the achievements of science and technology have fostered a sense in us that only what is visible and tangible, quantifiable and analyzable, is real. That may well account for much of the modern inability to believe in immortality. Yet we all experi- ence forces that, while invisible and indeterminate, shape and color, enlighten and enchant, our lives.

Love is such an invisible force. It certainly cannot be anatomized, or schematized, or reduced to clearly identifiable elements. Yet its impact is irresistible, and it holds the power to transform us.

Music is another such invisible force. Its source and its nature are mysteries even to the most profound composers and literate listeners, yet its ability to affect reality, even to help heal the diseased body and mind, is undeniable. The other arts, too, while perhaps less abstract in language, are no less intangible yet wholly real in influence. Coleridge once defined art as "the subjection of matter to spirit so as to be transformed into a symbol in and through which the spirit reveals itself." What a felicitous description of holy art! What a glorious definition of the holy life!

There are those who recognize this reality of the invisible. And there are those who even while they experience its force, do not grant it such recognition. Thus to some people, "a primrose by a river's brim, a yellow primrose is to him and it is nothing more." Another man has a clearer vision, so he finds "tongues in trees, books in running brooks, and God in everything." For the physicist, water is composed of two molecules of hydrogen and one molecule of oxygen—that is a scientific fact. But is this all we can say about water? Is this the sum and substance of its essence? Shakespeare, as we just heard, read "books in brooks," and Israel's sweet singer found firm faith "by still and stilling waters." Surely *their* discoveries are as real as the scientific formulas of the laboratory. Let us be in the company of those who discern such a deeper vision.

Aye, the invisible is real. We spend the better part, nay, the best part of our lives in the realm of the invisible. Then why not affirm that magnificent, invincible surmise that just as love abides, and goodness abides, and truth abides, our souls abide forever, too.

Not too long ago I was hospitalized following a severe heart attack. For long days and nights I was in the intensive care unit— not a pleasant place. My own pains and fears aside, its noises were not restful to the ear: the running feet of doctors and nurses, the creaking of machines wheeled in for some emergency, the moans and cries of pain . . . and on two occasions during my stay, the dances and the rattling of death, and then the weeping of the suddenly bereaved.

About a week after I arrived I had to have some tests, but the required machines were located in a building at the opposite end of the hospital campus. I had to be wheeled across the courtyard on a gurney, and as we emerged from our unit the sunlight struck me. Just that—that was the apex of my experience—the warm and sparkling and brilliant light of the sun.

I looked about me to see whether anyone else was relishing

the sun's golden glow, but all I saw were women and men and children hurrying to and fro, nearly all with their eyes fixed on the ground. I remembered, then, how often I, too, had been indifferent to the grandeur of each day, too occupied with trivial and sometimes even base concerns to respond to the splendor of it all.

"There are those who gain eternity in a lifetime," says the Talmud; "others gain it in an hour." I believe I regained my life and regained the "invincible surmise" of my soul's immortality just in that moment of commonplace insight: the insight that life is wondrous, that we dare never ignore its offerings, that we must seize each of its golden minutes with all our heart and soul and might.

This, then, is my strongest intimation of immortality: that the gift of life surrounding us is boundless, that each moment of insight is an eternity, that the here and the hereafter are one and the same in the human heart.

· 8 ·

Is There Life
After Death?

BLU GREENBERG

Blu Greenberg is arguably the single most beloved, respected, and renowned Jewish feminist thinker in North America today. A graduate of Brooklyn College and Yeshiva University Teachers Institute, she also holds master's degrees in Clinical Psychology from City University and Jewish History from Yeshiva University's Revel Graduate School of Jewish Studies.

Ms. Greenberg has through her personal example demonstrated the possibility of combining an Orthodox life-style with feminist values. In the process, she has raised up a generation of disciples who look to her as mentor and teacher.

Blu Greenberg has served as the president of the Jewish Welfare Board's Jewish Book Council of America. In addition, she has contributed her talents to the cause of Soviet Jewry, to Federation, to *Sh'ma* magazine as a Contributing Editor, to *Hadassah* magazine and the Jewish Publication Society as an Editorial Board member, and to the Center for Learning and Leadership (CLAL).

Not entirely trusting myself to deal with this topic, slightly fearful of it, and wishing to gain some distance on something so intensely personal, I decided first to interview several friends and relatives on their views of an afterlife. Below is the condensed version of two informal interviews. The first is of L., an Orthodox Jew, fifty-plus years old, a successful entrepreneur and highly intelligent man, and the father of three grown children:

B: Do you believe in *olam haba* (the world to come, the hereafter)?
L: Of course.
B: How do you understand or envision it?
L: (long pause) Now, that's a different story. I am not really sure.
B: Well, let's give it a try.
L: I see it in two ways. One, a place where the good people go or rather, where their souls go after they leave this place; and second, the way I say it every day (in the daily *Shemoneh Esreh*)—the resurrection of the dead at the end of days, whatever or whenever that is.
B: Let's go back to the first idea. So you believe there is some kind of universe where the souls of the righteous "live," so to speak?
L: Well, not exactly. When my father died (in his sixties), I thought his soul surely went to "heaven," that he lived on after his physical demise. Because he was such a good person, he should have lived another twenty years, so at first I couldn't accept that his life was over. Naively I kept thinking he was going to come back. But of course, he never did. . . . So I picked the most available concept, *olam haba,* and that is what I told myself. And that is what I told my kids, and that is what they believed—and maybe still do, though come to think of it, no one has mentioned "Grandpa in heaven" in a long time. But I believed it myself. Even now sometimes I believe my father knows what is happening on earth, what I'm doing, but only rarely do I think so. I certainly don't imagine there is a whole society of souls out there conversing with one another. I don't think my father's soul meets every day with [the souls of] his

cronies from his old shul. On the other hand, my mother says she talks to my father, and when she dies, God forbid, I think she will be reunited with him. But I suppose that contradicts what I just said [about souls getting together]. . . . I'm not sure how the whole thing works. I suppose I should study it. Who has written about this?

B: So, in other words, except for your mother's and father's souls reuniting, the main activity of a life after life, or a life in the world to come, is communication with those still in this life, a vertical form of communication connecting the two worlds, rather than a horizontal one with all of the good souls living on in *olam haba* and constituting a society of good souls?

L: Yes.

B: Am I putting words into your mouth?

L: No. That's exactly what I was saying.

B: What, then, does *olam haba* mean?

L: Something for the philosophers and halachists to deal with.

B: Let's go back to the personal for the moment. When you die, God forbid, and you pass the test of righteousness and warrant a place in *olam haba,* do you think your soul will live on?

L: No worry. I wouldn't pass the test. I'm an ordinary mortal.

B: But if you did?

L: I don't know, really; I just don't know.

B: Would you like it to be so?

L: I'm not so sure about that either. On the one hand, I am curious about people. It might be interesting to look on and know what is happening on earth, to keep tabs, to see how the kids and eventually the grandchildren are doing. On the other hand, I think a clean break between life an death might be good. I don't really know if I'd want to live on. Life is great, but when I die—hopefully not before another thirty years or so—sooner if I'm sick—when I reach eighty, I'll probably have had as much as I can stand. Besides, as I understand it, there's no food, clothing, and no sex, so what good is it? Just kidding; don't quote me on that.

B: Well, this is all anonymous.

L: Okay, then. Just kidding!

B: How about resurrection at the end of time? What's your personal view?

L: An even deeper mystery. Though I know it's one of our basic beliefs, physical resurrection is not central to my personal faith. I suppose this is why I have mixed feelings about autopsies. [L. believes, contrary to the view of many Orthodox rabbinic opinions of our time, that autopsies should be performed to help science advance in the task of saving future lives.] . . . But perhaps I'm too young and too far from the end of time and enjoying the good life here and now to answer those questions. . . . I guess in the ultimate economy of things . . . [these concepts are] necessary to human faith.

B: But why? In what way?

L: They give people an anchor or a dream that life isn't over when it's over.

B: But you just said you wouldn't necessarily want to live on.

L: Yes, but as I understand it, resurrection means the whole thing, physical bodies and all. And as I understand it, you don't have to pass any tests. Everyone will be restored to life, and goodness will reign, and there will be no evil or war, and people will be good and moral. And the *yemot hamashiach* [messianic times] is a good vision to have, something to hope for, better times.

B: Do these concepts have an impact on your personal life?

L: (long pause) I don't think so. Occasionally it has occurred to me that when I want to do something I know I could get away with that is evil, something that is truly evil, not just paying in cash with no sales tax, but something like murder or stealing or violence, that I will be punished for it in another life. But even then it's more a matter of God watching me now and holding me accountable. Still, I am not going to take any chances. So, I guess you could say it does have an impact in terms of preventing me from doing something really terrible. . . . But then, I'm probably unique in this, because if people in general understood this notion of punishment in

What Happens After I Die?

the next life, there wouldn't be as much evil and violence, raw evil, in the world today.

The second interview was with G., an Orthodox woman in her early forties, extremely intelligent, a mental-health professional, and mother of seven. It is presented here in abbreviated form:

B: Do you believe in *olam haba?*

G: Well, I know it is one of the thirteen Ikarim (Articles of Faith). Therefore, I have to believe in it.

B: What is it you believe?

G: In my naive way, I believe it is a place where souls are basking in the splendor of God, not in a corporeal way but in a spiritual sense.

B: Does it have an impact on your personal life?

G: Yes, though not in a conscious way. Or perhaps I should say I'm conscious of it in the abstract. I understand it as a reward, a reward for living the proper Jewish life. . . . I also like to believe that at some point dear ones will be reunited in some way with their loved ones. . . . But I don't believe it is only the righteous, only religious people, who will [merit this] . . . but all people leading a good life, the right kind of life, will live there. By that I mean people who do their best to live a good life. . . .

B: Is there a connection between this world and that, a consciousness between the two worlds?

G: It could be. I really don't have a sense about this.

B: Have you ever discussed the idea of *olam haba* with your kids?

G: I have on occasion talked to them about *olam haba,* but in terms of reward and punishment—no!

B: When you die, God forbid, and you qualify for a place in the next world, how do you conceive of it? What do you think it will be like?

G: I haven't come to terms with it. It doesn't have a subjective quality for me where you go, where the souls go, if one doesn't make it, what the relationship is between heaven and hell—these are things I haven't grappled with.

B: Is there any connection between heaven and hell?

G: I imagine there must be, but intellectually I can't grasp that concept. It's too simplistic to think there's one place for the good people and one place for the bad ones. It's far more complex than that.

B: What about *techiyat hametim* (resurrection of the dead)?

G: I don't have any idea.

B: Do you think your soul will live on?

G: If it does, it won't be in the form of a continuation of myself, not me functioning as a human being, as I do now or as I am now. Rather, it would be some distilled, clarified spiritual essence of myself. . . .

However, it seems to be in vogue now to believe in some kind of a concrete hereafter. I find it shocking, and very telling that recently one of the soap operas on TV featured a whole group of people in an afterlife. A few people died, and then they were in heaven, dressed in white, orchestrating what was happening here on earth—such as whether to avoid an accident that would kill someone, etc. Something like *Oh, God* [the movie]. . . ."

Coming back to what I said before about basking in the splendor of God, I believe there is some connection between learning Torah and that existence . . . that it will be some kind of spiritual existence. Maybe it will be so distilled that it will be just basking.

B: Just there, lolling around?

G: Yes, but I think there will be some sort of Torah enterprise, Torah emanations. If Torah is only for this world, then it wouldn't be so, but if, as I believe, Torah is something more, then whatever aspect of Torah is transcendent and beyond this world will be pursued in the other world.

I think it will also be some sort of perfect communal existence. I suppose the reason I say this is because of the midrash *"tzadikim*

nehenim miziv hashechinah," a picture of tzadikim sitting at the
table, learning Torah and basking in the splendor of God. Part
of that is the image of tzadikim not being able to flex their
arms and therefore unable to feed themselves so that each one
feeds the other across the table. To me that symbolizes a perfect
communal existence.

These ad hoc, unschooled, though very thoughtful eschatological
opinions reflect more or less the views held by other respondents:
a diffuse understanding of the tradition on matters; a range of
belief and disbelief in the hereafter—the odd combination of remote-
ness and immediacy, ambivalence and affirmation; and finally, a
very tenuous acknowledgment of the impact of such concepts on
one's actions in the present life. Moreover, these informal findings
parallel those of others who have looked at the state of contemporary
belief.[1]

Had I been similarly interviewed on the subject, without benefit
of preparation, as was the case for my respondents, I believe I'd
have made quite the same statements—ambivalent, hesitant, uneven,
of piecemeal knowledge. And this despite that I know the concept
of the afterlife is a staple of the faith system I fully embrace, high
up on the list of the top ten or thirteen principles the philosophers
and halachists select for their primary lists. It is an elemental belief
I liturgically affirm with regularity and without a second thought,
or to be more accurate, without a thought altogether.

However, when one is forced to take a long, directly focused
look—which writing forces one to do—one learns something else
about one's self. In the course of working on this chapter, I was
surprised to find how powerfully I hold a view of an afterlife and
how deeply and profoundly it influences so many of my decisions
and actions.

Having said that, I must convey the other, which is also true—
that despite its deep and pervasive impact, the idea of an afterlife
is not something I think about systematically or coherently or speak
about very often, if at all. This raises a curious question, and then
a second one:

Is it possible for one's actions to be informed by so inchoate a value, one not even close to the surface? Yes, I believe so. It is a value that is deeply internalized, securely embedded in the psyche; thus, it is ever ready to influence deed and thought. Nor is it mere rationalization to say that this is perhaps the most healthy way of incorporating such a belief. Were it ever present in consciousness, it would border on the morbid and exert a paralyzing effect. One should stay focused on this life and not become detached from it. To do otherwise would be to suggest that this life is unbearable; fantasies of an afterlife would then serve as ropes thrown overboard. Not surprisingly, as one chronicles through history the idea of an afterlife, it becomes quickly apparent that, when Jews (or Christians, for that matter) felt the noose around the national neck, concepts of afterlife and resurrection took on more prominence than in better times, when such ideas fell from dogmatic eminence.

Next question: If my thoughts of an afterlife are so diffuse, so far from surface consciousness, how is it possible for me to know that they affect my very life? One way is that this concept comes to the surface periodically, reflexively, intersecting my here-and-now life at strange times and in unexpected places. And it feels quite comfortable; I never fight it, never deny it.

One such example, an incident that occurred many years ago when I was a student at HILI yeshiva, comes to mind now. My ninth grade *chumash* teacher, Mr. Levy, had previously taught us: The whole world is like a vestibule. Prepare yourself in this world so that you may enter the world to come (*Pirke Avot* 4:21). I do not remember my initial reaction, but it wasn't something stunning. Probably I tucked it away quite matter-of-factly, as philosophically passive teenagers of yesteryear were wont to do.

Several weeks later, in one of those irreverent acts that thirteen- and fourteen-year-olds commit against vulnerable authority figures, we girls planned a mock wedding. When Mr. Levy turned the knob and walked through the classroom door, we surprised—no, shocked—him with shouts of "Mazal Tov" and a hail of confetti all over his dark blue serge suit. I see his face before me even now, the rounded features, his eyes opened wide in disbelief. The generally mild-dispositioned and slow-spoken Mr. Levy turned quite furious and then quite pale. For a brief instant, I feared he would die of a heart attack. Then the thought disappeared from my mind. But, through my tears of riotous laughter, I felt a momentary pang of remorse.

In five minutes, it was back to business as usual. Except for confetti all over the floor, smudges of wiped-off lipstick around our mouths, the bride's and groom's paraphernalia resting on a back desk, we were docilely back to the study of sacred texts. But I had had a flash of insight. I remember looking all around me. Was this room my vestibule?

I do not know whether this was the first time I experienced a glimpse or glimmer of an afterlife. Given my upbringing, I tend to doubt it, for surely, I, like L's young children, had had death explained to me in terms of an afterlife. Nor do I know how often thereafter I experienced my life as a vestibule. Certainly it was not a recurrent pattern, but I do know that every once in a while a palpable feeling that there is a real world beyond my immediate one is summoned from the recesses of my being and then returned to a quiet resting spot until summoned forth once again.

What triggers thoughts of an afterlife? A variety of experiences. When I hear of someone who has successfully made a *shiduch* or when I labor in the matchmaking field myself, I not only rejoice in the new couple's happiness but instinctively note that the matchmaker will be rewarded with a place in the world to come. When I make special effort to study Torah under pressured circumstances, I'm aware that my efforts will be rewarded with a place in the afterlife. When my mother-in-law, who survived her husband by fifteen years, would speak of her conversations with him, and then toward the end of her life speak of joining him, I would listen to her with wonder, not doubt.

Yet I must acknowledge that my most powerful and frequent thoughts of the afterlife arise from a different source. It is not the view of the afterlife as reward nor as image of a place for souls to be rejoined that trips the eschatological switch. Rather, the notion of an afterlife serves as an inhibitor of harmful, dishonest, or evil deeds, actions I might otherwise try to get away with, acts that I would not be held accountable for on this earth, things that no one would know but God and me, and which perhaps not even the heavenly computer is tallying at this very moment. There are situations where I could steal, not only outright theft, but where someone has given me too much money or has added up the columns incorrectly, and no one would know if I didn't speak up; situations where I could take revenge on someone who has hurt me and that person would never know it was I who had harmed him or her; or more base feelings—fantasies of wanting to murder someone and no one would suspect me because of the fine station in life or particular reputation I enjoy. Unlike L.'s case, the immediate consequences of my actions (such as fines, jail, or embarrassment) seem less significant than the consequences to my life after life. And unlike G., who doesn't think in terms of reward and punishment, I think of final judgment, tipped scales, divine retribution, full disclosure, total accounting. It is not that I am consumed with contemplation of a place in the world to come or even that I envision and long for it, but rather that I don't want to be unworthy of it; I don't want to fail the test for entry—I tremble at the very thought.

So I have admitted it: my primary and recurrent association with afterlife is its inhibition over my baser instincts, the fear of being found out at the end of my days. I am not necessarily proud of this, for I am aware it is a more primitive, less sophisticated, less mature view. Yes, I know we should exhibit virtuous behavior for its own sake, out of pure love for God and humanity, and not out of fear of punishment. Nevertheless, I am grateful that even an inchoate vision of the next life keeps me relatively "clean," free of moral stain, in this one. It is not totally foolproof, and happily my base instincts are less rather than more. Still, a final accounting before crossing into the afterlife is an important accessory to a large set of ethical laws for the here and now. Given the penchant for some evil in ordinary people like myself, there would surely be greater incidence of breach. Similarly, when I perform a good deed that goes unnoticed or unrewarded—as do many good deeds in life—a quiet awareness that this act will eventually be counted makes me feel good.

A second powerful association with afterlife comes when I am forced to confront death or injustice—even more so, when these two forces converge, such as in the untimely death of an unusually good person. Perhaps *olam haba* is not an immediate answer, nor even a fully satisfactory one; yet here, too, the image of an afterlife gradually assimilates itself into the subconscious and from there surfaces every so often.

Last year a dear friend died very suddenly. I felt a massive grief at his loss not only because I loved the man but also because of his death at this particular time of his life. Simmy, age seventy-four, had recovered from a nasty bout of shingles two years earlier. After years of urging by his wife, Anne, he finally agreed to semiretirement from his busy law practice in Boston, which meant he now worked only twelve hours a day. They had recently purchased an apartment in Jerusalem, directly across the street from their younger son, daughter-in-law, and four young grandchildren. The latter were very close to him and, like their father, called him "Dad." Simmy and Anne planned to spend several months a year in their Jerusalem apartment.

Simmy was a true *tzadik,* albeit in bon vivant's clothing. Courtly and polished, he could also be opinionated and contentious. Beneath that colorful exterior, beneath even an occasional goddam and what in hell, lay the gentlest, tenderest of souls. He did more acts of *chesed,* more favors for people, than anyone I've ever met. Any of his acquaintances who ever encountered an underdog would instinctively advise, "Go ask Simmy G. for help." And somehow he always managed to find a way to avoid even the merest thanks. He could have called in one-tenth of his personal IOUs—which he never had anyone sign—and lived out his years, unto one hundred and twenty, in luxury and dignity. Yet just as he was poised at a moment when he could finally enjoy a most happy time of life, it was snuffed out. He should have had another fifteen years, ten at least. I wept for a solid week after his funeral. I grieved for his wife, for his children and grandchildren, as did the many hundreds of people who attended his funeral and walked in his cortege, the great and famous rabbis who eulogized him, the bank clerk who burst into tears a week later upon learning of his death. For weeks and then months I grieved at the premature end of his life and could find no consolation anywhere inside of me.

More than any saint I've ever read or heard of, Simmy deserved a place in *olam haba*; by dint of a single act of *chesed*, the scales of the heavenly court would have been tipped, and he would have been sent express to the world of the righteous. Yet in the weeks and months immediately following his death, this did not once occur to me. He was dead, very dead. If he was not here, he was nowhere. It was totally unfair, unjust.

But my system simply could not handle that. It rebelled against so blatant a violation of fairness. In recent weeks, as the pain has become a bit less raw, as time has given a small measure of respite, I find myself occasionally thinking that Simmy is probably arguing and cajoling his way through heaven, helping a few helpless saints. And I've heard his extremely bright and sophisticated twelve-year-old grandson Noah say, "I talked to Dad. . . " All of this doesn't take away the sadness that he's not here, but somehow it makes it more manageable. Otherwise we might just throw up our hands in total bewilderment. . . .

These, then, are my primary associations with an afterlife. Still I have not answered for myself the question: why do I believe? Rational skeptic that I am, why should a matter so thoroughly unverifiable, so defiant of laws of nature, have penetrated my consciousness and exert such power over me? . . . I who read with great suspicion reports of those who have "been there and back," glowing whiteness, lightness, pervasive love. . . .

One reason, I am certain, is because I was schooled that way.

Olam haba, techiyat hametim, bet din shel ma'alah—these are prominent features of rabbinic literature, of liturgy, of *halachah* and *aga-
dah*. Educated as I was in Orthodox institutions where these concepts were—are—taught quite matter-of-factly and are never
challenged, I simply took it all for granted. Mr. Levy's classroom
appeared to me to be a vestibule because Mr. Levy had transmitted
the message of the sages that it was so. G's vision of *tzadikim*
feeding one another across the table was her association because
she had encountered that particular *midrash*. When I tell a joke, I
am mindful of the *halachah* that requires me to give proper attribu-
tion to its author. When I see a letter lying in a drawer and am
curious about its contents, I remember the ban: one who eavesdrops
or reads another's mail loses a place in the world to come. Such a
simple act made so explicit reverberates in my mind when I am
faced with the opportunity or desire to commit an even larger
"crime." Just as I have accepted the commanding voice in other
areas of Jewish living and belief, so, too, here.

The second reason I believe is that I think I must. For me, as for
many other people, the idea of a hereafter serves a cosmic need.
There is simply too much injustice in the world, as the old Yiddish
proverb "God runs the world but not like a *mentsh*" attests. If
God is omniscient, omnipresent, omnipotent, there has to be something else beyond this moment in time. Hitler now in his grave
and Jewish children now born to the second generation are not
enough. Hitler deserves something more terrible than inert death,
and the second-generation parents' one hundred cousins who didn't
survive deserve something more than our memory of their truncated,
traumatic lives. Nice guys should never finish last. And I have
seen righteous people neglected and their children begging for
bread, and I know something is terribly amiss.

The reader might question how I can give the second reason,
cosmic need, when I have just given the other, that I would not
have come to the idea on my own had I not been educated to
believe. Perhaps there is inconsistency here, yet both are true. After
having been educated to believe in *olam haba*, I find it natural to

apply that concept as an answer to questions that others who were not a priori disposed to that idea would try to answer in some other way.

Up until now, dear reader, I have told you I believe life doesn't end when it ends. I have also described what triggers a mental association with afterlife. Finally, I've attempted to explain how I came to such a belief.

But the original question was: what happens after we die?—a question that challenges me to conceptualize "life" on another plane of existence. The truth is that here I am not at all sure what I envision. Let me reflect on the matter a moment. It could be that only the soul lives on, embodied in some kind of vaporous matter. But, no, I don't think so. On the other hand, if souls are reembodied, flesh upon bones, at what state of physical development, or decay, does this occur? Surely our bodies are not resurrected in the state they were at death. . . . Who would want that? And, if it is bodies— as my nephew Nachie once asked, "Where's there enough room?— and, if the next world entails resurrection in bodily form, why do I feel no fear that I might exist in the world to come as a blind person because of the eye donor card in my wallet? I find myself in agreement with those halachists who legitimate selective autopsies as long as they meet the conditions that the body parts are treated with dignity and then given proper Jewish burial and that the accumulated knowledge will increase and enhance life on earth— for the honor of the living takes precedence over the honor of the dead. Yet who knows?

Will the bodies of those who die in the *galut* roll through subterranean channels until they reach the Holy Land and from there be restored afresh to a future life? Who is my late neighbor with now? Is he rejoined with his first wife who predeceased him by thirty-one years and who now lies next to him in the burial plot they purchased long ago through their synagogue, or will he ultimately be with his second wife of thirty years, whom he also adored?

Is the next world a parallel world, with communities or hierarchies—or is the only hierarchy the one that exists between heaven and hell? Is there gender equality? I wonder. Are people's feelings hurt? Does Noah work out the entire conversation, or is Simmy actually talking to him? Are my Uncle Isaac and Aunt Ceil, who were married, not too romantically, for almost fifty years and died within a few hours of each other and traveled together in short twin caskets from Seattle to Jerusalem, still bickering and still caring for each other? Is corporeal revivification a total impossibility?

And who gets in? Is it all Israel, except for a few sinners, or is it all the righteous of the world, including even those who believe in many gods yet affirm the afterlife?

And what activities abound in *olam haba*? Is it primarily Torah learning? Is my mother-in-law busy all day long acting as a *melitz yosher*, an intercessor on behalf of her numerous kin? Are there children running about, and are their youthful souls wafting about more energetically than the oldsters'? Is there eating and drinking? Can you taste a persimmon in the afterlife? Can there ever be a life without dieting?

I have a thousand questions, but only at this very moment. Otherwise I simply never bother to envision this realm. I can agree with almost any scheme that has been presented, as well as with its opposite. Through my interviews, I came to understand that this is true for others as well. Geniuses that the rabbis were, they constructed a philosophy of afterlife offering something for everyone—images to appeal to different personal world views and engage very different souls. Rejecting one eschatological scenario, an individual can find his or her resonant images in a different traditional source. The rabbis advanced a fundamental teaching that somehow remains responsive to personal packaging and to very individual taste. The only requirement, it seems, is that one affirm the idea. Beyond that, it is open season.

And that suits me quite well, for I am certain that what may have been an appropriate vision as a child no longer suits a mature adult. In fact, I would categorize my conception of life after death as a sliding scale of faith. As Arthur Cohen has suggested, belief in the hereafter is a "doctrine of trust, neither pressed upon others nor denied by ourselves."

All of which brings me to my final comment in this chapter,

though not likely my final thoughts on the matter: Perhaps I feel so little concern with detail and so much engagement with concept because the major impact of *olam haba* is on my life here and now, not in the sense of rerighting the scales of justice but rather as a paradigm for this very life. What the concept of revivification, resurrection, afterlife says to me is that you can fall down and rise up again. You can hit bottom and turn around. You can suffer depression and reversal—and spring back. Life inevitably has its swings, and just as some sort of physical life and the life of the soul can come back after death, so can life on this earth. It is no coincidence that in the *Shemoneh Esreh,* the blessing for resurrection incorporates concepts of lifting the fallen, healing the sick, freeing the trapped: it is the blessing not only of life after death but of optimism for better times in this life. Not only can God restore life after death, but the Holy Blessed One can lift us up, over and over again. And not only God, but you, I, can restore, renew, refashion our lives.

For that alone a belief in life after death is worth holding on to. Besides, the rabbis say, who does not believe in it will find no place in the world to come. I'm not willing to take any chances. I believe. I believe.

NOTES

1. See, for example, Arthur A. Cohen, "Resurrection of the Dead" in *Contemporary Jewish Religious Thought,* ed. Arthur A. Cohen and Paul Mendes-Flohr (New York: Scribner's, 1987), pp. 807–13.

See also Arthur J. Magida, "Is There Life After Life?" *Baltimore Jewish Times,* October 16, 1987; Claude Montefiore in his opening paragraph of "The Life to Come: Resurrection and Judgment" (Chapter 31) states, "[The rabbis] thought . . . in terms and conceptions most of which have become obsolete and remote for us today, and so their ideas are of small interest or profit." Claude Montefiore and H. Loewe, eds., *A Rabbinic Anthology* (New York: Schocken, 1974), p. 580. Even more surprising is that Christianity, with such a powerful model of personal resurrection, also finds its contemporary believers short on this subject.

· *9* ·

Immortality through Goodness and Activism

RABBI HAROLD M. SCHULWEIS

Rabbi Harold M. Schulweis is known and respected as one of modern Judaism's most insightful and creative thinkers. Born in New York in 1925, his background is a rich mosaic of various ideologies and environments.

Schulweis was raised in a Yiddishist Zionist household, influenced by Orthodox grandparents, trained in a Yiddish shule, a Talmud Torah, and an Orthodox yeshivah before his ordination at the Conservative Jewish Theological Seminary.

His thinking was shaped by writers as diverse as Y. L. Peretz,

Joseph Soloveitchik, Ahad Ha-Am, Israel Salanter, Martin Buber, and Mordecai Kaplan. This mosaic engendered his passionate commitment to Jewish pluralism, embodied not only in his writings but in his very being. Schulweis is identified as a Conservative Jew but extends his love and ecumenism to all things Jewish. His books and articles are read avidly by Jews of every denomination, and his visionary work as rabbi of Congregation Valley Beth Shalom in Encino, California, launched what today is known as the Chavurah movement.

Jews Rarely Speak of Life After Death

You ask me what I believe about the afterlife, and I in turn am
struck by the fact that yours is a question rarely asked by Jews. It
is different with Christian audiences, where inquiries about the
Jewish view of life after death are almost invariably the first questions
posed. How is it that as a rabbi called upon to officiate at funerals,
deliver eulogies, comfort the bereaved, I am rarely questioned about
the disposition of the soul after death or the place of heaven or
hell, or the belief in the physical resurrection of the dead? How
is it that in the discussions about the meaning of the Holocaust
and the destruction of one-third of our people, the Jewish position
on the hereafter plays no part?

How do we account for this neglect despite the prevalence of
the ideas of *Gan Eden* and *Gehinnom* (heaven and hell), *olam haba*
(the world to come) in the rabbinic literature of the Talmud, in
Jewish mysticism, and in medieval Jewish philosophy? Despite the
praises of God's "calling the dead to eternal life" in the daily prayer
book and the references to paradise (*Gan Eden*) in the *El Male*
prayer recited at the funeral and during *Yizkor* services, the afterlife
does not function as a major Jewish belief among modern Jews.

Judaism Stresses This World

The this-worldliness in modern Judaism is not devoid of traditional
Jewish roots. For one thing, the Five Books of Moses make no
explicit references to another world beyond the grave. The Bible
refers to the death of each of the patriarchs as his being "gathered
to his kin" (Gen. 25:8; 35:29; 49:29, 33). One of the psalms
recited in the festival *Hallel* prayers declares: "The dead cannot
praise the Lord, nor any who go down into silence. But we [the
living] will bless the Lord, now and forever. Hallelujah" (Psalm
115). Carrying out this theme, traditionalist Jews at the funeral
cut the fringes of the prayer shawl that is placed around the shoulders
of the deceased. That custom is explained as symbolizing the belief
that the deceased have no *mitzvot,* no deeds to be fulfilled. To be
alive is to have deeds to perform and imperatives to be followed.

Our Task Is to Fix This World

The emphasis in Judaism is on the exercise of human free will to mend the universe. The ambivalence toward otherworldly reward and punishment lies in the fear that it may be used to excuse lack of individual and social activism here and now. A story is told about a pious Jew who boasts to his rabbi that he had saved another Jew's soul. A beggar had asked him for a meal, and he agreed but insisted that first they must pray the afternoon *Minchah* prayers. And before serving him the meal, he ordered the beggar to wash his hands and recite the appropriate blessing and thereafter to recite the *Motzi* prayer over the bread. The rabbi showed his annoyance with his pious disciple. "There are times, my son, when you must act as if there were no God." The disciple, taken aback by this counsel, protested "How should I, a man of faith, act as if no God existed?" The rabbi replied, "When someone comes to you in need as this beggar came, act as if there were no God in the universe, as if you alone are in the world and that there is no one to help him except you yourself." The disciple asked aloud, "And have I no responsibility for his soul?" The rabbi replied, "Take care of your soul and his body, not vice versa."

The story expresses the apprehension that an exaggerated emphasis on spirituality, on God as provider and rewarder may paralyze the human spirit and rationalize passivity. So Moshe Leib of Sasov said that God created skepticism so that we "may not let the poor starve, putting them off with the joys of the next world or simply telling them to trust in God who will help them instead of supplying them with food."

Belief in a Hereafter Causes Great Dilemmas

There are other factors that may account for the modernist distancing of otherworldliness. Jewish philosophers such as Saadia, for example, deal with the hereafter of persons in a literal and materialistic manner. Coping with the belief in the physical resurrection of the body, Saadia wonders what happens to the injured or amputated body, or to the person's body devoured by a beast or cremated. How will the resurrection take place? Will the injury to the body be healed? Will the people resurrected be able to exercise free will and sin? If so, will they be punished, and, if not, then are they without free will?

This sort of materialistic literalism led to strange and unappealing speculation. In this connection, modern Judaism favors a more symbolic and poetic interpretation of the hereafter. Heaven and hell are not geographic places but states of mind, ways of living rather than spaces beyond the earth. The attention shifts from place to time, from "where" to "when." Not "where" is heaven or hell but "when" is it experienced.

When Is Heaven?

Consider the legend of a good man who after his death enters heaven and is disappointed that there are no "saints" there. He is informed that he is mistaken. The "saints" are not in heaven. Heaven is in the saints.

In a complementary story, a chasidic rabbi is asked, "Where is God?" He answers, "Wherever you let Him in."

So, in discussing—in a moment—the meaning of the immortality of the soul, we shall refer not to "where" the soul is but "when" the soul exists, not to the biology of the soul but to its morality.

Life Is Our Responsibility

In Judaism the extraordinary emphasis on life in this world makes a second life elsewhere appear as pale compensation. Death is regarded by some Jewish thinkers as an insult, a contradiction to the purpose of religious life. The mourner's act of tearing a part of his clothing, they suggest, expresses anger at this assault upon life and its promises. We recall that in the *"Chad Gadya"* hymn sung at the Passover Seder, the Angel of Death is slaughtered by the God of life, an echo of Isaiah's prophecy, "He will destroy death forever; the Lord God will wipe away the tears from all faces" (Isaiah 25:8).

The Nobel literary prize winner S. Y. Agnon suggested that the *Kaddish* the mourner recites to magnify God's name is meant to console God, for the loss of a human being diminishes the strength and glory of the Creator. The mourner's *Kaddish* itself speaks not of death or of another world but of life in this world and in our time. The ritual of the *Kaddish* calls for a *minyan*, a living community of at least ten Jews, to honor the deceased. So the memory of the deceased depends on the presence of life.

In matters of faith such as that of the afterlife there are no scientific or logical proofs. If "seeing is believing," what is it we are looking for in speaking about God, soul, immortality, resurrection?

Science measures and weighs what is, faith is concerned with what ought to be.

Following that distinction, we may find a clue to the beliefs about the afterlife. What fears and what yearnings of the spirit in this life go into the belief in the continuation of life after death?

The hope for life after death may be related to our discontent with the status quo. The world in which there is so much poverty, war, illness, a world in which innocence suffers and wickedness prospers cannot be the last word of God. Seen in this light, *olam haba* (the world to come) expresses a protest against the injustices and imperfections of this world. In Judaism this world and everything in it is far from perfect. As the Talmud puts it, the grain needs to be ground, the bitter herbs need to be sweetened, the soil must be plowed, "everything requires mending."

There is a huge gap between the world as is and the world that ought to be. That vacuum is filled by belief in another world in which to live. For some, then, belief in another world is driven by the conscience to compensate the victims of this world. Yet, for others, otherworldliness is suspect lest it be exploited by those who seek to delay forever the tasks of this people, this day, in this world.

The rabbinic tradition tries to hold on to both worlds, to counter both the seduction of passivity and the submission to the status quo. Consider the surface paradox taught in the *Ethics of the Fathers* (*Pirke Avot,* or *Avot*):

> Better is one hour of repentance and good works in this world than the whole life of the world to come; and better is one hour of bliss in the world to come than the whole life of this world.   (4:17)

On a more personal level, let me relate the interactions of traditional Jewish wisdom and my own experience. My grandmother died three days before the festival of Sukot. The funeral was held, the mourning period, normally seven days in duration, began, but in accordance with Jewish ritual law, once the festival began, the mourning ended. The tradition is clear: *Haregel mevatel gezerat shivah*—the festival annuls the mourning period. I was at first somewhat resentful that the personal mourning of the family was subordinated to the public celebration of Sukot. But as I thought about the ritual rule I sensed the wisdom of the tradition. My grandmother was a devoted Jew, and she would not wish to disturb her people's joy. (In Yiddish she would say: *"nisht farshteren die simchah."*) The consolation came from the shared conviction that her immortality was bound to the eternity of our people. Individuals die, but *ein hatzibur mait*—the community does not die. Eleven months after her death that faith was inscribed on my grandmother's headstone. It read, in the traditional expression, *tehei nishmatah tzerurah bitzror hachayim*—may her soul be bound up in eternal life.

What Is the Soul?

But what is her "soul"? I do not understand soul as a material object but as an expression of her life. She was a woman of kindness, gentle in speech and manner, a woman of charity who baked and cooked for sick and poor, who blessed her household as she closed her eyes and raised her hands before the lit Shabbat candles. I still call to mind her counsel, her embrace, her charity. She created memories that inform my life and helped shape my values. In that sense, my grandmother enjoys an immortality of influence. In speaking of her soul I mean those godly qualities in her personality that transcend her bodily existence and affect the character of those she touched.

There is a parallel here to what we learned in physics as the principle of the conservation of matter. That principle maintains that the sum total of the energy of the universe neither diminishes nor increases though it may assume different forms successively. Analogously the spiritual energy expressed during our lives—the wisdom, goodness, and truth of our lives—does not evaporate into thin air but is transformed into different forms of thought, feeling, and behavior and is transmitted through our memory: the conservation of spiritual energy.

In thinking back on the deaths in my family and among my friends, I sense in the belief system and ritual practices of our tradition two important gestures, two complementary ways of looking at death and beyond it. The two require the art of holding on and letting go.

> Hold on and let go
> On the surface of things contradictory counsel.
> But one does not negate the other.
> The two are complementary,
>   two sides of one coin.
>
> Hold on—for death is not the final word
> The grave is not oblivion.
> Hold on—*Kaddish, yahrzeit, yizkor.*
> No gesture, no kindness, no smile evaporates—
> Every embrace
> has an afterlife
>   in our minds, our hearts, our hands.
>
> Hold on—and let go.
> Sever the fringes of the *talit* and
> the knots that bind us to the past.
> Free the enslaving memory that sells the future
>   to the past

Free the fetters of memory that turn us passive,
listless, resigned.
Release us for new life.
Lower the casket, the closure meant
to open again the world
of new possibilities.

Return the dust to the earth
not to bury hope
but to resurrect the will to live.

We who remember are artists, aerialists
on a swinging trapeze
    letting go one ring to catch another.
Hold on and let go
    a subtle duality
    that endows our life
    with meaning—
Neither denying the past
    nor foreclosing the future.
We are part of the flow of life
    the divine process,
        which gives and takes
creates and retains.
We, too, must give and take, seize hold and release.

The Lord giveth and the Lord taketh
    Blessed be the Name of His Sovereign Glory.

(Poem by author)

Personal Epilogue

To ponder what I believe will be the essence of my immortality is an invitation to write my own obituary. The challenges are two-fold: to filter out my conceits and to try to remember the future. I invite the reader to attempt the same exercise.

A celebrated comedian concluded his monologue on the afterlife with the roguish punch line: "I believe in my immortality, but I want it while I'm still alive." There are indeed intimations of im-mortality I have experienced while yet alive. Whenever I see my granddaughter cover her eyes before the Sabbath lights and

hear her sing-song the benedictions in Hebrew, I sense a transcendent joy quite different from that derived from her recitation
of a nursery rhyme. It is not the curtsy "cuteness" of her lisped
recitation or her precociousness that touches me, but in her benediction lies a shock of recognition. This benediction I heard chanted
by my grandmother and mother. It is intimately associated with
my family and the warmth and festivity of the Sabbath table. This
blessing is a nexus, a sacred connection between my ancestors'
world and that of my grandchildren. Hearing it from my grandchild,
I know that I am not alone in my future. My Jewishness is validated
not only by the origins of my past but by the continuities resonating
in my grandchildren. I am not only descendant but ancestor of
my tradition.

Additionally I have been blessed with a vocation that brings
me into the lives of others. People come to me sharing their most
intimate concerns. They come with fears, ambitions, disappoint-
ments, and I am privileged to think with them, to cull insights
from the wisdom of our tradition, and to disentangle the knotted
skein of their anxiety. Years later I hear from some of them sentiments acknowledging my help. Therein abound hints of something
personal that lives beyond the grave.

One particular project I was privileged to institute ties me with
both my people and the future. In 1987, I founded the Jewish
Foundation for Christian Resources, devoted to searching out,
identifying, and helping those non-Jews who risked their lives rescu-
ing persecuted Jews during the dark years of the Holocaust. History
occurs, but not everything is automatically inscribed in its books.
Not history but human beings record events. Unreported, the most
important episodes in life are as if they never happened. Unrecorded,
the good are robbed of their just immortality. The rescue behavior
of non-Jews who reached outside the circle of their own faith to
rescue Jews hunted by the Nazis has regrettably not been systematically researched. If that situation is not remedied now, humanity
will be denied important evidence of goodness lived and practiced
even in the hell of Auschwitz. The past has to be properly remembered so that the future may be properly changed. I believe there

are sparks buried in unrecorded history that must be freed from the caverns of amnesia. Moral archaeology, digging out the nuggets of supreme value from the past, helps shape a more balanced and wiser theology for the future. Discovering and understanding the flesh-and-blood heroes of our tragic past may provide models and motivations for the generations after the Holocaust.

Immortality, mine, my people's, and others, refers to something indefeasible, something sacred that will not be trampled underfoot. I hope—don't we all?—to leave a shadow on this earth to offer testimony that I have lived. For all his humor the comedian may have been right in his desire to have immortality here and now. It's a question of knowing where to look for it. A legend tells of the angels who were jealous that God was to create the human being in God's own image. That image is immortal. God and his human creations would share immortality. Why, then, were Adam and Eve so anxious to eat from the tree of life—the tree of immortality—after they ate from the tree of knowledge? Because they learned that the angels plotted to hide it from them. One angel proposed that immortality be hidden from them in the mountains or the seas far beyond the reach of man or woman. But others argued that human beings would climb the mountains and plumb the oceans to find it. Then the shrewdest angel of all suggested that immortality be hidden within and between human beings. That angel surmised that within and between would be the last place on earth people would search to discover eternal life, now that we know the secret. Immortality is within and between us, and its intimations are here and now.

· *10* ·

Covenant Theology
DR. EUGENE B. BOROWITZ

Dr. Eugene B. Borowitz was born in 1924 in New York City, the son of Benjamin and Mollie Borowitz. The family moved to Columbus, Ohio, where young Eugene received a Jewish education in a Conservative synagogue. Borowitz first began to think about becoming a rabbi in high school, when he wrote a letter to the then Hebrew Union College. He was ordained in 1948 and two years after ordination returned to the college to pursue a doctoral degree. When the Korean War intervened, Borowitz became a chaplain and finished his doctorate while in military service.

Borowitz entered congregational life, subsequently joined the staff of the Union of American Hebrew Congregations, where he rose to the position of director of the Reform movement's Commission on Jewish Education, and ultimately joined the faculty of the New York Campus of the Hebrew Union College-Jewish Institute of Religion. He has served and taught there with distinction for close to three decades.

In order to understand an individual's belief in the hereafter, it is necessary to survey this person's overall philosophy of life. For Eugene Borowitz, the following thoughts represent the context out of which his notions of death and afterlife emerge.

To Be a Jew

For me, being a Jew is fundamentally a religious matter, one that derives from the ongoing validity of the people of Israel's historic relationship with God, the Covenant. The classic Jewish books, the Bible and the Talmud, testify to this assertion, for they center about God and the service due God. Until a hundred or so years ago, it did not seriously occur to many people that one could be a good Jew without believing in God. If anything, belief in God was so much a part of Jewish life that one did not need to talk much about it. Though often unspoken, everything else in Jewish life depended on it. Thus, the weight of Jewish history, tradition, and practice connects believing in God with being a good Jew and opposing theories must bear the burden of demonstrating their Jewish authenticity.

I also find that the passage of time has lessened the once nearly universal opposition by liberal Jews to the notion that a good Jew believes in God. Since the 1940s ended, we no longer consider atheism great sophistication. Even the agnosticism that allowed us to dispense with God because we trusted culture wholeheartedly increasingly shows its obsolescence. A spiritual shift has begun among serious Jews in our community, and a growing number can now speak of God in personal ways that would have made us uncomfortable some years back. With our new appreciation of the extraordinary openness with which Judaism has allowed people to talk of God, "my" good Jew believes in God but not necessarily in my view of God. We have numerous differing interpretations of what God might mean to a contemporary Jew, and in my several books I have tried to help liberal Jews understand the various modern notions of God, from rationalism through existentialism and on to religious experience and beyond to mysticism. (Eugene B. Borowitz, *Liberal Judaism* [New York: UAHC, 1984], p. 130).

The Covenant

For me, the ideal Jew cannot be someone who believes in God but has no concern for the Jewish people—as some among us once contended—nor someone who loves Jews and Jewish culture but denies or ignores God—as did the Yiddishists and classic Zionists of yesteryear and the Israeli nationalists of today. Only in the relationship between God and the Jewish people, the Covenant, does authentic Judaism appear. My good Jew, then, believes in and lives in the Covenant (Borowitz, *Liberal Judaism*, pp. 132–33).

Liberal Jews consider Torah historical but not time-bound. We associate it particularly with Mount Sinai, but we understand it also as a continuing creative stream of Jewish spiritual search and self-expression through the ages. We know it can find authentic forms in modern times as it did in yesteryear. Often the tales and practices from ancient times and distant places not only express our Covenant sentiments but instruct us in their proper depth. Sometimes continuity falls short of our needs or even impairs living out our faith. Then out of our immediate sense of Jewish duty to God as part of the Jewish people we creatively add to the repertory of Jewish teaching and living.

As to beliefs, then, I see a good Jew having a living relationship with God as part of the people of Israel and therefore living a life of Torah. Three major areas of Jewish responsibility arise from this situation.

First, the Covenant obligates Jews to sanctify their lives and their relationships with others. Of all such duties, none has a higher place than that of being ethical. We may even say that this command rests more heavily upon Jews than upon all humankind, for the Jewish people claim to represent God in history. The primacy of ethics in Jewish duty flows naturally from the faith that all humanity has but one God and that God "cares" about nothing more than that people treat one another with righteousness.

Other duties flow from grounding one's life as a Jew upon God's reality: daily prayer, study, and religious observance. The week moves toward Sabbath observance; the year is punctuated with

Jewish holy days; each life has its beginning, end, and other major moments marked by special rites. All these events have more than purely personal significance. They have a communal dimension, for life under the Covenant involves the Jewish people as well as God. The Jewish family provides the critical link between the individual and the folk at large, so Jewish duty largely centers on participating in a rich Jewish family life. A good Jew participates in synagogue, for there the community regularly renews the Covenant through liturgy, deepens it in study, and refreshes it by association. That institution, in turn, leads Jews on to serve the Jewish community locally, nationally, and worldwide—and through it, all humankind.

Ours being a time of special Jewish peril and attainment, the good Jew will be especially concerned about the survival of the Jewish people everywhere, most particularly in the State of Israel. The Holocaust mandates an overriding Jewish concern for other Jews. We cannot depend on others always to be of help to our tiny people. So wherever a Jew cries out for help—Argentina, Iraq, and most dramatically recently, in the Soviet Union—other Jews need to be listening and active in their response. Or, more positively put, a good Jew ought to support every activity that upbuilds and enriches Jewish life anywhere (Borowitz, *Liberal Judaism,* pp. 134–35).

God

Though I try to teach Jews about the many ways of thinking about God in contemporary Judaism, I have my own position among them. People have relationships that are deeply significant for their lives without fully or nearly understanding those with whom they have such relationships. I find the personal the best model we have for talking about God. As against rationalist models, concepts of God (clear intellectual envisagements of God) are of subsidiary interest in traditional Judaism—if not positively discouraged. Making concepts of God primary tends to make thinking about God a substitute for relating to God and implies the human mind is capable of apprehending God. In a relationship, thought is not abandoned, but it must not dominate. It serves as a critic of faith and as explicator of its consequent responsibilities. This is the safeguard against superstition and cultism. At the same time there is openness to many forms of envisaging God. That is, any concept of God that makes relationships possible (or is appropriate to living in Covenant) is acceptable here. This seems closer to the traditional model of agadic thinking than liberal theologies have been in prior generations as a result of their emphasis on an idea of God as the essence of Judaism. And it provides for continuing intellectual growth in our understanding of God, a characteristic of all of Jewish history, particularly in our time.

The perception of a transcendent demand upon us to preserve the people of Israel, the affirmation of a transcendent ground of value in the face of contemporary nihilism, have led many Jews to a restoration of the relationship with the other partner in the Covenant, God. The absence of God and the hurt we have felt are not intellectually explained. Yet it is possible, despite them, to continue the relationship. For the intellectually determined, the most satisfactory way of dealing with this issue is to say God's power is limited. For those to whom this raises more problems than it solves, there is acceptance without understanding. Both positions are compatible with relating to God in Covenant. I find myself constantly tempted to the former though mostly affirming the latter, a dialectic I find appropriate to affirming the Covenant (Borowitz, *Choices in Modern Jewish Thought* [New York: Behrman, 1983], pp. 283–85).

Who and What Am I?

For all that I am intricately related to my body, I know myself to be a person and not merely a chemical structure. I do not say I have a "soul," a term heavy with Greek philosophic and medieval metaphysical overtones, for in today's culture I would not know how to substantiate the existence of such an entity. Still, there is something about me that enables me to share in God's reality. I know a bit about God. At my best, I consciously serve God, and my acts help complete God's work of creation. I occasionally have a glimpse of what God wants of me and of all humanity. Sometimes I am capable of rising above the frailties within and social ugliness without to dedicate my life to a purpose far transcending my small existence. This exalted human capacity deserves as much attention as does the chemistry of our life stuff—or more, for it is what makes us characteristically human. And it is the experiential base of our sense that we are like God and thus may be privileged to share in God's eternal life.

Naturalism, the modern intellectual current dominating America at midcentury, hoped to find what is truly real by reducing everything to its smallest physical constituent. The other view, mine, and I think that of Jewish tradition, sees reality most clearly in the most complex thing we know, a person. The one perspective breaks everything down to impersonal energy. The other says we see ultimate reality more clearly as we build upward from human nature to what transcends and fulfills it. If God is the most real "thing" in the universe, then we may hope that, as we make our lives ever more closely correspond to it, we may personally share God's eternity despite our death. And knowing ourselves to be most fully human through our individuality, we trust that the God who is one will preserve our oneness and grant us personal survival after death (Borowitz, *Liberal Judaism*, p. 221).

We Do Not Understand Death

Don't try to imagine what it's like being dead. (I'm not yet talking about life after death.) In the first place, whatever you come up with has to be awful. Death being the opposite of life, as far as we can tell, all you can imagine is different kinds of nothingness. The point is, however, you won't "be" dead. Think about it: When you're dead that means "you" are dead and you won't "be" or "feel" anything, not even bad. The words "being dead" make no sense together. If you have "being," you're not "dead." Either there is some sort of life after death, and "being dead" means what you're doing in that existence, or else you're dead, in which case "you" won't know it. So you can stop trying to figure out what it's like to be nothing.

This discussion already illustrates the problem with this topic: How do you talk about something you've had no experience with? As difficult as it is to discuss God we can say that through our minds or in our lives we've had some personal sense that God is real. How can we think about death? All we know is life. The closest thing to death in life is sleep—only we are very much alive when asleep though not very conscious of it. How can we figure from life its opposite? Death is a real mystery, one none of us can avoid, and that makes it frightening (Borowitz, *Understanding Judaism* [New York: UAHC, 1979], p. 217).

Death Is a Mystery

Death is a great mystery. We do not know life without a physical base. We have no experience of what existence the other side of death could be like. Against that ignorance we balance our recognition that life itself is mysterious, that death is part of life and the creation God ordained. Death, like life, comes from the God who we know daily showers goodness on us. We trust God's goodness even in death. We cannot believe that, having shared so intimately in God's reality in life, we do not continue to share it beyond the grave. Our creaturely existence, which enables us to rise to the level of participating in the ultimate reality in the universe, God's, now may aspire to extend and fulfill that greatness we came partially to experience in life. Having reached such heights precisely in our personhood, our individuality, we likewise trust that our survival will be personal and individual (*Reform Judaism Today*, Book 2: "What We Believe" [New York: Behrman, 1977], p. 48).

Life After Death—A Personal Statement

As a liberal I am dedicated to humankind's significant role in achieving God's purposes. With that sense of faith, I am unlikely to give up my activism and patiently wait for the life of the world to come. True, because I do not consider people the only agents of fundamental change, I will not bring a messianic enthusiasm to every immediate social struggle. But should my projects fail, I will not be as dispirited as many onetime liberals have now become. Believing there is only one life, they have grown discouraged, even bitter, because they were not able to bring the messianic age in their time. Often they now despair of human progress altogether. Why should they spend their only existence suffering continual defeats, why sacrifice their precious few years to the painful task of resisting evil?

Believers who do not expect vindication in this life alone are saved from the spiritual rot that easily sets in when humanity proves obdurate to change or malevolent in interest. They trust God to reward them in another existence for what they have suffered for God's sake in this one. They may even be strong enough to see their defeats on God's behalf as joining them to God's reality. Their lives will be fulfilled no matter what happens in this world, for they have a life with God yet to come. And, trusting God, they know history will one day be redeemed by the One who will not ultimately be defeated.

I do not know much more than that, how I shall survive, what sort of judgment awaits me, or what I shall do in eternity. I am, however, inclined to think that my hope is better spoken of as resurrection rather than immortality, for I do not know my self as a soul without a body but only as a psychosomatic self. Perhaps even that is more than I can honestly say, though in the use of this term I may lean upon Jewish tradition with which I share so much else. Ultimately I trust in what I have experienced of God's generosity, so surprising and overwhelming so often in my life. In such moments I sing wholeheartedly the last stanza of the hymn "*Adon Olam*": "In God's hand I place my soul both when I sleep and when I wake, and with my soul, my body, God is with me. I shall not fear" (Borowitz, *Liberal Judaism,* p. 222).

· 11 ·

Outrage and Faith

ARLENE AGUS

Arlene Agus, born into an observant family in Brooklyn, New York, was educated at The Yeshiva of Flatbush. The Orthodox environment in which she was raised at home and in school imbued her with a love of Judaism and of Israel and a desire to ease the suffering of Jews in need. The example provided by the rabbis and philosophers in her own family—past and present—was one of personal responsibility for perfecting all areas of human life, in the Jewish community and beyond.

One of the founders of the Jewish feminist movement in the United States, Ms. Agus has promoted women's scholarship

116

through learning centers and study groups, including the Drisha Institute. Her work in immigrant policy, nuclear ethics, and Jewish culture has made Ms. Agus one of the Jewish community's most sought-after lecturers.

In synthesizing her spiritual life, feminism, Zionism, and social activism, Arlene Agus stands as a role model for many young women.

In 1944, at the height of World War II, my father and his buddies prepared to fly overseas. After nine months of rigorous training, they awaited their B-25 transport with both eagerness and apprehension. One week before their departure my father was stricken with an illness that grounded him, forcing him to remain behind as his crew went on to Europe. He was never to see them again. Two days after they left he received a call from the base: the B-25 was lost over the Atlantic. All of his buddies were dead.

My father later recovered and went on to serve the army until the war was over. But the question that arose then still lingers to this day: What was it that had saved my father's life? Was it simply luck? Coincidence? Or—as I eventually came to believe—*hashgachah peratit,* divine providence, that intervened to spare him?

Fifteen years later my father was a successful accountant with a wife and two growing daughters when suddenly, for a second time, illness struck. This time, however, it was not to be a temporary setback, but Parkinson's disease, a chronic, degenerative syndrome that gradually makes you a prisoner inside your own body.

That was thirty years ago. By now my father lives in a nursing home; my mother, having spent three decades caring for him—as well as for my sister and me—is ill as well. When I look back over the events of this man's life, I still cannot make sense of them. Why did he escape an early death during the war only to spend a lifetime in suffering?

I have asked my father how he himself understands his life. You should know that he is a simple man, not particularly given to philosophizing. So you can imagine my shock when he replied, "My sickness is a punishment." "A punishment? For what?" "The Holy One is punishing me for my sins." "But, Dad, you are not a sinful man; you are a good man. How can you believe God would do this to you?" Unshaken, he said, "Surely I have sinned. I accept my fate without complaint."

Well, perhaps my father can accept his fate stoically, but I certainly cannot. I am furious. I am outraged. I challenge God to explain, to correct this unfairness. It seems to me that dignity is the very birthright of those created in God's image. Dignity cannot be realized without the unfettered freedom to think, to choose, and to act. But this freedom is the first victim of such tragedies as have befallen my father and countless others. How can we come to terms with such events and with the God that sees them?

I know that there are those, like my father, who believe in a stern God of justice who expects a higher standard of morality from His followers than from others and who exacts punishment accordingly. That God is not my God.

There are others who believe in a good but limited God who created the world but is unwilling or unable to intercede in its history. That God is not my God.

Mine is certainly a good and just God, infinite in knowledge and power, and without form or gender. [Though God is genderless, English pronouns are not. With reluctance I will use the masculine pronoun "He" for linguistic simplicity, echoing the generic form of the Hebrew.] But above all He is purposeful, and His purpose is inscrutable to human beings. And though evidence of God's presence and testimony to the existence of a cosmic plan is abundant, like the weave of fine lace, the full pattern of that plan depends on the intricate interaction between the visible and the invisible, the tangible and the imagined, the revealed and the implied. I cannot understand how God can "hide His face" from us—*hester panim*—in the face of evil, nor can I fathom why suffering has a place in the divine design. All I know of God is what He chooses to reveal.

I believe in this God not because it is expected of Jews or because it is comforting, but because I myself have perceived Him, because I have felt His hand guiding the course of my life.

In addition, I have come to know God as He is manifest in the world around me. I encounter Him daily in the products of the first six days of creation: the heavens and the earth and the seas, living creatures and plants that grow from the soil. I have learned what God expects of me through the holiness I experience as I pray or study sacred texts. Finally, I witness the role of God in history—in the record of life contending with death, progress vying with retrogression, good competing with evil.

I know what God has revealed. What I want to know is *why*. Why did He choose to create a world? And, knowing that people would inevitably confront suffering in it, why did He choose to create human beings? Why did God create in us aspirations that our circumstances would prevent us from attaining? Why would He instill in us the longing for dignity and then force us to confront poverty, physical handicap, or oppression?

Why grant us the faculty of reason when our fundamental questions about life itself would remain forever beyond our reach? "Why did you beckon to me, wondrous shores," asked Hebrew poet Rachel, stricken with tuberculosis at an early age; "why did you disappoint me, distant lights?"

The anger that I feel as I pose these questions dates back to the very first Jew. Our patriarch Abraham challenged God on what appeared to be His decision to destroy the righteous along with the sinners of Sodom and Gomorrah. Abraham knew it to be the right of the created to have a voice, to make demands, and to hold God to His own standards of justice.

There is a curious passage in the Talmud, Tractate *Eruvin* 13b, recording the conclusion of a debate on the question of whether it would have been better had God never created the human race. Astonishingly the rabbinic majority concluded that it would, indeed, have been better had we not been created. They went on to say, however, that since we find ourselves here, our task must be to aspire to worthwhile goals.

And for most of my life I agreed with that view. I, too, felt that the suffering endured by most people on earth could not justify the good life enjoyed by the rest of us. It was a lonely and tormenting position to hold. In addition, it left the basic contradiction unresolved: If God really was wise and good, as I believed, how could I maintain that He'd erred in bringing human life into being?

Over time, though, an experience I'd had in high school began to take on increasing importance in my thinking. It happened during a lesson taught by one of my many teachers who had survived the Holocaust in the context of explaining to our yeshivah class how his beliefs had withstood the unimaginable evil he had witnessed. He held up a Spalding—a pink rubber ball that fit into the palm of his hand—and asked what we saw. "A ball," we said, rather annoyed at the question. "Describe it," he said. We described a perfect pink sphere. He asked, "How do you know? Can you see the entire ball?" We had to concede that some part of the ball was always hidden from our view; still, what we saw of the front implied a matching shape and texture on the back.

And that was precisely what he was trying to demonstrate: if we could not even see the entirety of a familiar physical object, how could we expect to see the full dimensions of the divine plan? If on this small scale things were hidden from us, how much more so the fundamental order of the universe.

Thus was born my belief in an afterlife. If God was true to His nature, He would have answers. He would have reasons. But He—not I—would choose the appropriate time to reveal them. It was this little pink ball, then, that gave me the patience to wait for answers and to temper my outrage with humility.

My love for God is a bit like human love; I do not need to know everything about Him in order to trust Him and extend Him credit. A worthy loved one will always repay one's trust.

Every morning we say, "You have created my soul, formed it, breathed it into me; you keep body and soul together. One day You will take it from me and restore it to me in the hereafter." I take this promise literally. In the relationship described in the Covenant, God provides us with raw material, and with it we are to construct our lives. We are given freedom of choice in *olam hazeh*—this world—and the work of our own hands will determine our fates in *olam haba*—the world to come.

Naturally, I cannot paint a picture of *olam haba* or describe it in any concrete way. I know no more about it than you do: no more than any living person and no less than the greatest philosopher. Even so, I cannot resist the seemingly childlike hope that after I die I will be reunited with my grandparents and others I have loved, and have the opportunity to study Torah with Moses. But most of all I want my mother and father to be compensated for the crushing hardship of their lives. I want to finally hear the *why* explained to me by God himself. As a religious Jew, I cannot imagine myself without these expectations.

The afterlife is not simply a psychological crutch with which we appease ourselves. Nor is it a theological stick with which we threaten those who perpetuate evil. It is, rather, God's commitment to us, part of His responsibility as our Creator. By endowing us with souls, with aspirations, and with the potential for perfection—characteristics that have no limit—He has indicated that He intended us to be infinite, to exist beyond our physical lives. For me that belief is as fundamental as the belief in God. You cannot have one without the other.

But I cannot prove these matters of faith in any of the conventional ways we recognize as proof. People can rarely prove the beliefs they cherish. How do you prove that all people are created equal? That slavery is immoral? That feeding the hungry is a virtuous act? To me these truths are self-evident, as clear as though they'd been proven by scientific experiment or logical argument. So it is with religious belief.

In this way, outrage and faith coexist in delicate balance—the one forcing us out of complacency into lives of value; the other leading us forward, like the Israelites' pillar of fire, stretching us beyond ourselves and promising to reward our journey.

Outrage preserves our dignity, the dignity of the mortal whose nature inclines to rebel against finitude and despair. Faith represents the divine spark in all humans that burns upward toward its source and helps us to strain toward perfection. Together outrage and faith impel us to strive to the limits of our given abilities and leave the rest to God.

Trusting in God in this way frees us to concentrate on the immediate duties of the here and now. Just as we live in the tension between outrage and faith, so we live in the tension between present and future, this world and the world to come. And though we are destined for eternal life, Judaism cautions us not to dwell upon it, not to muse excessively on the imponderable issues it raises, but instead to give pride of place to the present and to make of our earthly behavior proud reflections of our Maker.

The temptation to give primacy to the future is offset in Judaism not only by this emphasis on the present but also through the counterweight of the past. Contemporary Jewish thinkers, such as Rabbi Eliezer Berkovits, underscore the unique relationship that exists between Jews and time. In this view Jews are able to withstand repeated historical calamities because they are firmly anchored in both their memories of past suffering and in their belief in future redemption.

Just as Jews appropriate the future as a source of strength, so do they mine the past for sources of inspiration. Just as we hope to be reunited with Jews of every epoch in the afterlife, so we are instructed to imagine that they and we were present together at Mount Sinai for the revelation of the Law.

Perhaps no element of Judaism so crystallizes the interconnection among past, present, and future as the family. In my case, we trace our family tree back nine hundred years to the great scholar Rashi. We also observe a family tradition of gathering once a year to mark a historical event with a festive meal and the reading of a special scroll. The scroll tells of another of our ancestors, the Chief Rabbi of Prague, who was sentenced to death in 1629. He had been wrongly accused of slandering Christianity, and although political intervention was successful in lifting his death sentence, he was heavily fined and forced out of his position. A genealogy appended to the scroll contains the family tree, listing the names of nearly nine centuries of ancestors. Through this story, solemnly recounted aloud year after year, the historical victimization of the Jews was made very real and personal to me.

In Rabbi Heller I had a specific name and face to stand for all the generations of anonymous Jews who'd been threatened with personal and communal destruction. Perhaps even more moving to me were those lists of names, individual people who lived real lives, Jewish lives, and passed their values down to me like a mandate. Their values became my values; their commitment to Jewish survival, mine as well. I devoted myself to Judaism—the motivating force behind the noble and ordinary lives that comprised my own inheritance. As the Israeli poet Yehuda Amichai writes, "All the generations before me contributed me bit by bit . . . like a house of prayer or charitable institution, my name is the name of my donors. . . . It binds."

Now living in a comfortable environment, free to practice Judaism openly, I feel inextricably linked to generations past and to those yet to come. I try to understand how my ancestors carried out their vision of God's commandments and how I should carry out mine in twentieth-century New York.

At rare moments I think I know . . . particularly on Yom Kippur. I stand waiting to pray before the ark wrapped in my *talit,* my head covered almost completely by its woven fabric. I can see no one. As I wait for the room to quiet down I think of the *Musaf* service I am about to begin. The first prayer is *Hineni,* an appeal to God and the congregation to overlook my personal limitations that I may serve as an emissary for the group's prayers. "Here I am," the prayer begins, "poor in deeds, trembling in Your Presence, pleading on behalf of Your people Israel even though I am unworthy." I close my eyes. I hear the dimming sounds around me representing the diversity of my community.

Tomorrow, I fear, we may repeat the mistakes of yesterday. But today we are solemn and repentant. Today, more than at any other time, we are aware of God's power and of the possibility of perfection.

I am awed by the responsibility of pleading the congregation's case before God. Each year I am struck by the extraordinary difference between Jewish and secular models of justice. In civil courtrooms two sides enter as opponents, each side trying to prove its point at the expense of the other. Divine justice is different. Here, the judge, the jury, and those appearing before the bench are all on the same side. All of us seek the same goals: to turn ourselves from deeds that make us less than we could be, to grant us life that we may begin anew.

The silence in which each of us concentrates during these prayers is not peaceful but rather tense and expectant. As I chant the part of the prayer that confesses my sins to God, I am aware that all my friends are listening. Suddenly, as they are uttered out loud, the impersonal words "we have sinned, we have transgressed" become "I have sinned, I feel ashamed." Yet I go on chanting, knowing this is not the time to focus on myself. Instead, using the same words being uttered in the same spirit in synagogues around the world, I try to elicit some reaction from God, a sign that we are indeed transforming ourselves on this day, a sign that we will be forgiven. And sometimes it will happen. A veil will lift, and I will feel a Presence. But even when no response is evident, I am united in purpose with the hundreds of people in the room whose voices engulf me as they join in the familiar strains of the *Kaddish*.

It is a time for infinite expansions. We are praying not only for ourselves personally or for our own communities or even for all Jews but for all humankind.

Musaf ends; the afternoon passes in prayer. And as the metaphoric gates of heaven begin to close at dusk, I perceive God reaching down to us as we reach up to Him. And as the distance between us narrows I am flooded with an exquisite mixture of feeling: fulfillment and yearning, humility and hope. "You are the force that created us," I say. "Will you grant us the longings of our souls and the healing of our bodies? Will you finally bring peace to Israel?"

The old sense of outrage begins to stir within me. *"Why?"* I start to ask, as if for the first time. But now God is listening, compassionate, making His mighty presence felt as though He were visible. And though I am no closer to the answers, the closeness to the One who knows them stills my outrage, restores my faith, and secures my trust. Another year may pass with only one side of the ball in view, but I have brought my earthly burdens to heaven's door, and I feel relieved and exhilarated.

I turn back toward my friends and reenter the sacred life of the ordinary. Which, after all, is where I belong.

· 12 ·

Death and Afterexistence:
A Polydox View

DR. ALVIN J. REINES

Dr. Alvin J. Reines, professor of Jewish Philosophy at the Hebrew Union College-Jewish Institute of Religion in Cincinnati, has become known as one of the most brilliant yet challenging thinkers of the modern period.

Reines, educated in Orthodox Jewish religious institutions and a descendant of a family that includes eminent rabbis such as the founder of the Mizrachi, an important Orthodox Zionist organization, had originally intended to enter the Orthodox rabbinate. Influenced by his studies in philosophy and psychology, Reines in time came to the personal conviction that Orthodox Judaism was based on beliefs that were untenable when critically examined.

Upon graduation from Yeshiva University, Reines determined to pursue his studies in a liberal Jewish environment suitable to an inquisitive mind and open to critical thinking. He was ordained from the Hebrew Union College-Jewish Institute of Religion in Cincinnati in 1952, received a doctorate in Philosophy from Harvard in 1958, and has touched thousands of students with his challenging ideas in subsequent years.

In 1970, Reines and a group of his disciplies founded the Institute of Creative Judaism, a research and development institution that publishes the liturgy, philosophy, and educational materials emanating from Reines's philosophy of Reform Judaism as a polydoxy.

The belief a person holds with respect to the question of afterexistence—that is, whether there is human existence after death and the form it takes—is intrinsically related to the particular religion to which one adheres. Hence it is necessary to preface this presentation of my view respecting afterexistence with a brief description of my interpretation of Reform Judaism, the religion of which I am an adherent. The reader will notice that I state "my interpretation of Reform Judaism." This phrase is significant. The reason is that no single or formal definition of Reform exists on which all members of the Reform community agree. There are, accordingly, different definitions or intepretations of Reform Judaism. This being the case, individual Reform Jews' views on afterexistence can, and often do, disagree as well.

Reform Judaism, as I define it, is a polydoxy.[1] Essentially this means Reform Judaism is a religion affirming the principle that each of its adherents possesses an ultimate right to religious autonomy or self-authority. Thus Reform Judaism affirms the right of all Reform Jews to act as their own ultimate authorities in determining their religious beliefs, and this entails the fundamental right to determine their own beliefs with respect to the question whether there is an afterexistence, and if there is an afterexistence, the form it takes.

Thus there are significant substantive and procedural consequences for Reform Jews regarding belief concerning an afterexistence when Reform is defined as a polydoxy.

1. There is no particular belief or dogma in Reform with respect to the subject of afterexistence that is incumbent upon Reform Jews to accept.
2. So far as Reform is concerned, no individual Reform Jew's view regarding afterexistence is more valid than any other's.
3. No reason exists for individual Reform Jews to enter into controversy with one another over whose belief is the correct one or the "true Reform" belief. Every Reform Jew has a right to her or his belief; no one's belief is "more" Reform Jewish than is another's; and no Reform Jew has a right to impose her or his belief on others.

4. The only reason for Reform Jews to hold a belief regarding afterexistence is that they wish to do so. Reform does not require its adherents to have any belief concerning afterexistence or even to think about the subject at all.

The nature and significance of the Reform Jewish position on afterexistence is thrown into bold relief when contrasted with that of Orthodox Judaism. In Orthodox Judaism there is a particular belief (dogma) regarding afterexistence that every Orthodox Jew must accept as true. This dogma is resurrection,[2] the coming to life of persons after death as they existed before death—namely, with the same minds and bodies. Along with the dogma of resurrection are included beliefs in a theistic God's judgment of the persons resurrected (dispensation of reward and punishment for the deeds performed by the person before death); sublimation to heaven (*olam haba*);[3] and hell. The Orthodox Jew who denies this eschatology is guilty of heresy and condemned for this sin to the punishment of eternal annihilation. In Reform, on the other hand, there is complete freedom to respond to the question of afterexistence as one chooses. There is no heresy or sin regardless of the decision that is made.

The Jewish Treasury of Afterexistence Concepts

It is all very well to say that individual Reform Jews possess the ultimate moral right to believe whichever concept regarding afterexistence they personally find convincing. It is, however, a daunting task for individuals to create de novo the many possible afterexistence concepts to consider before making a choice. This is the reason study of the Jewish religious past is of such great value to the Reform Jew. It is no overstatement to say that each of the major concepts regarding afterexistence has at one time or another been explored and believed in by some Jewish religious community or individual thinker. The past is a storehouse of Reform Jewish options regarding afterexistence belief. Before stating my own view, the following brief summary of the afterexistence concepts proposed by other Jews will show the reader the rich variety of choices open to Reform Jews. At the same time, this summary catalogs the views, which, except for one, I have considered and rejected.[4] Even though rejected, profound religious concepts that have been examined and evaluated in depth enrich the psyche.

There are no agreed-upon terms among philosophers and theologians to refer to the positions enumerated below, but in this presentation a term once defined will be employed consistently in the sense given. One preliminary point remains to be made. The concepts regarding afterexistence enumerated, excepting finitism, all refer to existence after death that is personal—namely, what exists after the death of a person is an entity consciously aware it has the identity and continues the individual existence of the person it was in its earthly life before death. Thus personal afterexistence excludes such notions of afterexistence as: "living on after death in the memory of others"; "living on after death in the accomplishments that survive one's death"; "living on after death through one's descendants"; and similar views.

1. *Immortality:* a concept of personal afterexistence in which the soul or mind survives the death of a person's body.
2. *Resurrection:* a concept of personal afterexistence in which the identical mind and body of the person who has died, as originally joined, come to life again some time after the person has died.
3. *Sublimation:* a concept of personal afterexistence in which a person's mind and body jointly survive death in a transfigured, nobler, more spiritual form. Sublimation can take place after resurrection. After resurrection the persons die again and experience sublimation. Resurrection and subsequent sublimation are basic beliefs of Pharisaic (Orthodox) Judaism. (Many persons believe that resurrection and sublimation are the original Jewish concepts regarding afterexistence. This is incorrect. The afterexistence belief of the Pentateuch [Torah] and Sadduceeism, both of which antedate Pharisaism, is finitism, which is discussed below.)
4. *Sheolism:* the concept of personal afterexistence that persons

after death continue to exist in Sheol, which, in the Bible, is taken to be the abode of those who have died.

5. *Transmigration:* a concept of personal afterexistence in which the soul passes at death from the body that has perished to another body.

6. *Afterexistence agnosticism:* the view that belief about a personal afterexistence is to be withheld on the basis that there does not exist competent evidence upon which to make a judgment.

7. *Finitism:* the concept that neither the mind nor the body of the human person survives death. Death is the end of individual personal existence. Finitism differs from afterexistence agnosticism in that the former makes a definite judgment that there is no survival of personal individuality after death, whereas the latter states there is no knowledge regarding personal afterexistence enabling a decision one way or the other. Finitism can include such sentiments as "living on after one's death through one's children or through good deeds," inasmuch as such sentiments do not signify belief in a personal afterexistence.

Religion and Afterexistence

As has been stated, there is no obligation in Reform requiring a Reform Jew to deal with the question of what happens after death. A Reform Jew can choose any of the alternative views on personal afterexistence enumerated above, but the choice exists not to think about the subject at all. Should a Reform Jew then confront the difficult subjects of one's own death and afterexistence? My personal conviction is that one should, and the reason is based upon the fundamental concerns of the human person and the nature of religion as I understand them to be.

Religion, in my view, is defined as: "the human person's response to the conflict of finitude."[5] This definition is based upon a concept of the human person as possessing two constituent fundamental elements in conflict with each other. One of these is awareness of oneself as pervasively finite; the other is a passionately intense desire to be infinite. Although I believe these two existential elements are present in the human person from the earliest stages, the age at which they attain a significant place in consciousness varies with the individual. By the human person being "pervasively finite" I mean the powers of humans are limited to the point where they fall short of every conceivable or imaginable standard of perfection. To illustrate this point: the human intellect cannot attain complete understanding of the universe; a perfect intellect would. The human mind and body are subject to disease and aging; a perfect mind and body would not be. Probably the most striking instance of human finity is the fact of death, the person's limited power to exist. Although finite, the human person, consciously or unconsciously, possesses a profound desire to be infinite—namely, to know all there is to know; to be mentally and physically invulnerable; and never to die.[6] The human conflict between awareness of one's finity and the longing to be infinite is referred to as "the conflict of finitude." The conflict of finitude left unresolved produces within the person feelings of angst and melancholy that drain human existence of meaning. This state of meaningless existence is termed "asoteria."

The deeply painful state of asoteria produced by the conflict of finitude gives rise to an urgent demand within the person to respond to the conflict and thereby resolve it. Successful resolution of the conflict of finitude brings the person to a state of ultimate meaningful existence, termed "soteria." The human response to the conflict of finitude is what I define as religion.

There are, I believe, fundamentally two valid responses to the conflict of finitude: the infinite response and the finite response. Although there are different kinds of infinite responses, all share the fundamental and essential characteristic of denying that death is the end of human existence, and all affirm belief in some form of personal afterexistence.[7] By believing in a personal afterexistence, a person resolves the conflict of finitude. The conflict of finitude, as stated above, is produced by the anguished clash between people's awareness of their finity and their yearning to be infinite. Accordingly, by believing in a personal afterexistence, people reject the awareness that they are finite and affirm that, on the contrary, they are infinite. There is then no conflict between what such persons now believe themselves to be—namely, infinite—and their intense desire to be infinite. They are what they passionately long to be and thus attain soteria. It is true that not all concepts of personal afterexistence provide everything infinite desire can imaginably wish for; each concept does, however, offer what humans yearn for most: infinite personal existence, and so, soteria.

The finite response to the conflict of finitude is basically the opposite of the infinite response. In making a finite response to the conflict, persons affirm as true their awareness of themselves as finite. This then clashes with the infinite desire within them. Thus, to resolve the conflict these persons must renounce infinite desire. Renunciation means acceptance of the limits bounding human existence, the reshaping of infinite desire into finite desire, and, in particular, reconciliation to one's death. By renouncing infinite desire, the will of these people to live is now a wish for finite existence, the existence they affirm they possess. Such people are now what they wish to be, the conflict of finitude is resolved, and with the resolution of the conflict soteria is attained.

The fundamental conclusion to be drawn from the foregoing discussion of the nature of religion is that whichever belief regarding afterexistence a person adheres to, the person can attain soteria. Whether one believes in eternal personal afterexistence or that personal existence terminates at death, one can achieve ultimate meaningful existence. It is, however, also clear from this definition of religion that failure to deal with one's finity—in particular, one's own death—leaves unresolved a human's fundamental existential problem, the conflict of finitude, and invites the continuing haunting presence of asoteria.

The point has been emphasized that in Reform Judaism all beliefs regarding afterexistence are valid, which is not the case in authoritarian orthodox religions. In such religions as Orthodox Judaism, Roman Catholicism, and Sunni Islam, not only is belief in a personal afterexistence obligatory but belief in a particular kind of personal afterexistence. Hence adherents of Reform Judaism do not have the problem that can confront orthodox religionists—namely, that of being unable to accept as true their religion's obligatory beliefs respecting afterexistence, which constitutes sin, and thereby induces guilt. For Reform Jews have the moral right to determine for themselves what their beliefs shall be regarding afterexistence. Yet Reform Jews can experience a problem with regard to belief in afterexistence: this is not conflict with their religion but internal conflict, one they engage in within themselves. Perhaps the form such conflict takes most frequently is this: Reform Jewish adherents come to the conclusion intellectually that they are in fact finite, and death consequently means the end of personal existence, but nevertheless are unable to give up infinite desire for eternal personal afterexistence. Such people are not at war with their religion, Reform Judaism, but with themselves. Internal strife of this nature obstructs resolution of the conflict of finitude and, to be dealt with productively, requires disciplined introspective and volitional effort.

Reasons for Believing in Personal Afterexistence

We arrive then at reasons why Reform Jews might believe in the survival of personal existence after death. These reasons are, of course, not necessarily exclusive to Reform Jews. There are only a limited number of reasons for belief in personal afterexistence, and historically these have often been shared by a number of different religious communities. Not all possible reasons for personal afterexistence will here be presented, only those that appear relevant to the present-day Reform community. Since Reform Jews enjoy autonomy with respect to beliefs relating to afterexistence, they have a right to choose whatever reasons they find convincing to support their beliefs. Consequently, I am presenting these reasons for the purpose of discussion, although my view is that they are either philosophically, psychologically, or scientifically unsound. Yet it does not matter if Reform Jews find one another's reasons unconvincing inasmuch as they have no right to impose their reasons for belief or disbelief on others who can simply reject them as unsatisfactory.

The reasons enumerated below stand alone, but some believers in personal afterexistence employ more than one.

1. Acceptance of hearsay evidence in which one person is told by another that the latter has firsthand experience or convincing evidence of some other kind proving there is personal existence after death. People who base their belief on hearsay evidence have no evidence for the belief other than someone else's unsupported word.

2. Acceptance of some document (such as the Bible) as infallibly true in which it is stated there is a personal afterexistence.[8]

3. Belief in a theistic God who exercises a just providence over humankind and therefore sees to it that every person is rewarded for good deeds and punished for evil ones. Inasmuch as it is evident that many good persons in this earthly life suffer undeserved misfortune and many evildoers enjoy undeserved prosperity, it is evident that many persons die without receiving their merited rewards and punishments. Consequently, since the theistic God is just, there must be a personal afterexistence in which all receive their proper rewards or punishments.[9]

4. Belief in a theistic God who is infinitely good and merciful and thus grants all humans a meaningful personal afterexistence.

5. Experiencing one's soul or self as having lived before in a different body or bodies at a different time or times; and concluding from this that one will again live in another body after the present body one occupies perishes.

6. Having an experience in which one has communicated with a person who has died. This experience may have come about directly or through a medium.[10]

7. The belief that the individual human intellect could not learn all the thought it creates or comes to know in a single lifetime, and therefore concluding that the intellect must have existed

What Happens After I Die?

prior to the body as a disembodied soul in a spiritual realm
where it acquired the knowledge it displays during its earthly
life.[11]

8. Belief without any evidence in a personal afterexistence simply
because one wishes to or because it makes life more meaningful. The notion is sometimes added that a person may as
well believe in a personal afterexistence, for if the belief turns
out to be wrong, nothing is lost, and meanwhile one has
been made happy in this life by the thought.

Finitism

My position is finitism; I do not believe there is a personal afterexistence. When I die, my individual identity will be annihilated, and
both my psyche and body will perish. I would like to expand on
my belief in finitism with respect to two points: why I believe
finitism is true; and the implications of finitism for a view of deity.

With respect to the truth of finitism, as with any belief, the
first decision to be made is whether to require evidence in order
to accept the belief as true. Then, should evidence be required,
what kind of evidence must it be? For myself, my decision is that
I only accept as true a belief that is supported by evidence; and
the evidence I require consists of either a sensum (plural: sensa)
or selfum (plural: selfa). A sensum is a perception experienced
through one of the five senses; a selfum is an apprehension experienced through introspection. Broadly stated, sensa provide information concerning the external world, or not-self, and selfa provide
information concerning the internal world, or self. Bear in mind
that decisions regarding what constitutes evidence are based on
arbitrary individual choices, and people will differ in their choices.
Thus, for example, I accept sensa alone as providing information
about what exists in the external world. Others, however, contend
they receive information about realities in the external world
through means other than the five senses. (Examples of this: some
people claim they apprehend the "presence" of a deity through
means other than the five senses; others claim they experience extra-

sensory perception.) Disagreement among members of a polydox community over the evidence each requires for belief about afterexistence and the different resulting beliefs presents no difficulty since each individual possesses an ultimate right to religious autonomy.

Having said this, I will examine briefly the reasons for belief in a personal afterexistence enumerated above, and indicate why none meets the standard of evidence for belief that I require.

1. Since I require the personal experience of apprehending a sensum or selfum as the only competent evidence for accepting a belief as true, I reject hearsay evidence as incompetent. I accept no religious belief on the basis of evidence someone else has experienced and I have not. (It is overwhelming to contemplate the myriad of individual religious experiences—often contradicting one another—one would have to believe by affirming the validity of hearsay evidence.)

2. Historically, the Hebrew Bible, particularly the Pentateuch (Torah), has been the primary document for which the status of infallible revelation has been claimed. Upon critical examination of the Bible, however, I find (as does critical scholarship universally) this claim cannot be supported. My conclusion, therefore, is that the Bible is the product of human minds and, therefore, fallible, for human minds are inherently limited and subject to error. Consequently the Bible cannot provide infallible evidence for any belief. Furthermore, even if the Bible were taken as infallible, nowhere is the concept of a personal afterexistence presented as a dogma of any form of biblical religion.

3. The view that there is a theistic God who exercises a just providence over humankind, which is the basis of the third reason given for belief in a personal afterexistence, must itself first be shown to be true before it can be employed as evidence to prove there is a personal afterexistence. My own examination of the facts of existence leads me to conclude theism is untrue.[12] Consequently, since the notion of a just providence requires the premise of a theistic God, I do not accept the

argument that there is a just providence requiring a personal afterexistence.

4. Just as my theological examination of the facts of existence leads me to the conclusion that there is no theistic deity who exercises a just providence, so do I also conclude from these facts that there is no theistic God out of whose perfect goodness personal afterexistence is bestowed upon humankind.

5. Upon thorough introspective examination I find no evidence that I possess a soul that previously occupied another body. Since I do not accept hearsay evidence, I give no credence to those who claim to have such a soul. Hence I reject the notion of transmigration and find it, therefore, no justification for belief in personal afterexistence.

6. I have had no experience of communication with those who have died. The reports of others who claim to have done so I reject as hearsay evidence.

7. The explanation for the remarkable accomplishments of the human intellect that it preexisted the body as a disembodied soul in a spiritual realm requires the existence of both disembodied souls and a spiritual realm. Since I have evidence of neither, I must reject this explanation of intellectual activity. (Please note that such an explanation raises more questions than it answers. We begin with the problem of explaining human knowledge and find ourselves with two far more abstruse problems: explaining the existence of disembodied souls and of a spiritual realm.)

Why Death?

The reasons I accept finitism and reject belief in a personal afterexistence are now clear. The only position for which I have credible evidence is that death brings to an end the psychic and physical existence of a human being.[13] I am not unmindful that the idea of personal afterexistence is a more pleasant fate to contemplate than is the personal annihilation of finitism. Authentic religious belief, however, does not consist of what one wishes were true of reality but of what credible evidence establishes as true of reality. Yet belief in finitism does not mean the end of thought about death. Profound metaphysical and theological questions arise from the fact of human death. In my view, the most fundamental of these is: Why death? Why does earthly human existence come to an end?

The classic theological explanation of the reason for human death appears in Genesis.[14] It states there that the god Yahveh completed creation of the universe by bringing forth Adam and Eve, the first humans. Yahveh then placed Adam and Eve in the garden of Eden, where he provided for all their needs. He made all kinds of beautiful trees grow in Eden whose fruits were good to eat. A restriction, however, was placed upon the fruits that Adam and Eve were permitted to eat. Yahveh commanded them:

> From every tree in the garden you
> are free to eat;
> but from the tree of knowledge of
> good and evil you must not eat.[15]

Adam and Eve, however, disobeyed Yahveh's command not to eat of the tree of knowledge of good and bad. For their disobedience Yahveh imposed a number of punishments on them. Moreover, these punishments were not limited to Adam and Eve but were extended to all their descendants. Among these punishments was that Adam and Eve and all their descendants must undergo death:

> By the sweat of your brow shall you earn your living until
> you return to the ground, since it was from it that you were
> taken. For dust you are and to dust you must return.[16]

The theological justification expressed in Genesis for the origin of human death may be phrased this way. There exists a creator God of the universe, Yahveh, who has the power to grant to humans eternal life without death. For the sin of Adam and Eve, however, Yahveh imposed upon all humans the punishment that they must undergo death. What this Yahvistic view comes to, therefore, is that there is a theistic deity who can bestow upon humans eternal life without death but who has chosen not to as a continuing punishment for the sins of Adam and Eve.[17] In sum, the creator God has the power to grant to human beings a richly meaningful eternal life without the plethora of evils that beset them but by divine choice refuses to do so.

My notion of God, generally stated, belongs to what are characterized as "finite God" concepts. Very different views of the nature of God are included under the rubric of "finite God" concepts. What they all have in common is the belief that whatever deity may be, deity is not omnipotent. In my view of the finity of God, divine power is limited to the point where God is incapable of being the ground (cause) of any kind of existence other than finite beings. It is not, therefore, humans alone who are finite, but everything that exists is necessarily finite, from subatomic particles to galaxies and the universe itself.[18] Accordingly, human death is not the result of divine punishment but the result of divine finity. There exists no deity who can bestow upon humankind eternal blissful life without death but who withholds this paradisiacal life out of divine displeasure with the first humans. Rather there is a finite deity without the power to give humans more than the limited existence they have. Finitism, understood in the light of a finite God, is not then the forced acceptance of the vengeful decree of a wrathful God, but the shaping of one's will to the reality of a finite deity who has no more power than to be the ground of beings subject to death.

NOTES

1. Alvin J. Reines, *Polydoxy: Explorations in a Philosophy of Liberal Religion* (Buffalo, N.Y.: Prometheus Books, 1987), pp. 24ff.
2. See "Resurrection," pp. 21–34 in this volume.
3. Ibid.
4. The concepts enumerated are discussed in some detail in other sections of this volume.
5. Reines, *Polydoxy,* pp. 63ff.

6. The particular infinite desires referred to here are, of course, not the only ways in which infinite desire can be experienced. Other particular infinite desires can express the basic general infinite desire.

7. As enumerated previously, pp. 130ff.

8. This is the primary reason for belief in a personal afterexistence in such religions as Orthodox Judaism, Roman Catholicism, and Sunni Islam.

9. This reasoning is somewhat similar to an argument formulated by Kant.

10. A medium is also referred to as a "channel."

11. This reasoning reflects a Platonic position.

12. Reines, *Polydoxy*, pp. 168ff.

13. I reject the view of afterexistence agnosticism that there is insufficient evidence upon which to make a decision regarding afterexistence; all credible evidence supports finitism.

14. Gen. 2:7–3:24.

15. Gen. 2:16ff.

16. Gen. 3:19.

17. Even those who believe in a personal afterexistence agree that a person must first undergo death.

18. See Reines, *Polydoxy*, pp. 176ff.

· *13* ·

Two Personal Statements

From time to time as we worked on the manuscript for this book, many friends asked us if we planned to share our personal views of life after death. At first, we determined not to do so. We finally realized, however, that we had an obligation to engage in the same sort of thoughtful introspection that we hope this book will stimulate in you.

Rabbi Daniel B. Syme

One of my most frightening daydreams as a teenager involved life after death. Frequently the thought occurred that one day I would die and the world would simply go on and on and on—without me. I was terribly bothered by the notion that my own life seemingly meant very little in the larger world of the universe, time, and space. In a very real sense, perhaps, I confronted the finitude of which Dr. Alvin Reines speaks so eloquently and was terrified by it.

I no longer have the recurring anxiety of my adolescent years. To a certain extent I have resolved the challenge that confronted me. We cannot *depend* upon the existence of a life after death. We have no way of *proving* or *disproving* that once we die there will be anything else. Therefore, for me at least, the only course to be followed is to live this life as though it were the only one. If there is a life beyond the grave, it will come as a wonderful surprise. If there is not, I will at least have the satisfaction of knowing that I did not live my life on earth in anticipation of another world but rather firmly rooted in this one.

There are some who feel that life, being so short, should be lived to the fullest, purely in pursuit of personal pleasures and with little or no regard for others. Others believe this life is given to us primarily in trust, for the sake of serving those besides ourselves, our own pleasures and satisfaction being inconsequential.

I have tried to live my life somewhere in between these two extremes. On the one hand, every day is a new adventure. On the other, I believe there is a duty we owe to future generations of the Jewish people. There is something each of us can offer to that future. In ways large and small, acts that we perform during this lifetime can make a difference in the next generation, even though we may not be here to see their ultimate impact.

First and foremost among the gifts we give to the future are our children. To the extent we see to their Jewish education, to the extent we imbue them with values of decency and kindness, to that extent do we attain a sort of immortality through their lives and the lives of those they touch.

A second way in which we touch the future is through our work. I have been fortunate in that I have had an opportunity to write books and articles for children and adults, part of whose content may touch and transform a life along the way. Again, I may never know it, but the existence of that tangible evidence of having lived gives a personal sense of meaning to my life.

Finally, we touch the world through kindness and caring toward other human beings, primarily the members of our own family, but the extended family of humanity as well. Each of us as individuals affects eternity. We never can tell where our influence stops. And we never can know when a touch, a caring word, an arm around the shoulder of one in pain, might stimulate that individual in turn to similar kindness or great accomplishment.

In short, since the existence of an afterlife cannot be *assured,* I choose to embrace a life here on earth that is as full as possible of elements of caring, concern, creativity, and love. If we are finite, I will leave this world knowing I have done as much as I possibly could to make it a bit better as a result of my having lived. And if there is a world hereafter, I imagine I will be living to the fullest "there" even as I have tried to in this world.

But while I have my own ideas of life after death, I often share those of other thinkers with people in pain. Perhaps the most touching is a legend shared with me by my father.

Franz Kafka once wrote an essay in which he described his feelings about the death of his sister. She was sixteen years old when she died, and Kafka tells how he was unable to find any comfort or consolation. She was so pure, so good, so kind. He asked himself how God could take this child. Why?

One day, Kafka says, he walked into a kabbalistic shul, where a group of mystics were discussing their concept of life after death. He listened intently as they described the next world where, they affirmed, there are ten spheres.

At the very center, said the mystics, is God and all the righteous. And then, in each progressively larger sphere, are millions and millions of souls. When a person is about to be born, a soul is sent from one of these spheres to join the body. The soul is told: "You have twenty years, or eighty years, or sixty years. At the end of that time, you will be recalled. If you have influenced the body toward goodness, you will be promoted from the tenth sphere to the ninth sphere. Then you will return to God or to the next world and after a brief respite be sent down to earth again."

The goal of each soul is to progress from the tenth sphere to the very central sphere. Then the soul no longer has to return to earth. It finds eternal peace.

This theory helped the mystics understand life. When you meet people who are very cruel or selfish, they said, don't criticize them too much. Perhaps they weren't lucky. They may have received a soul from the tenth sphere. Or when you meet people who are very kind, very compassionate, who are very giving and generous, don't praise them too much. Perhaps they were lucky and got a soul from the third sphere, which had already been down to earth countless times.

And then the Kabbalists said, when a young child dies, don't cry too much, because in all likelihood that soul needed to come to earth for just a brief time in order to be purified so it could join God in paradise.

Kafka concludes the essay and says, "I walked out of that shul and for the first time I had peace of mind. Now I knew where my sister was."

This legend is only a legend. But when we deal with the unknown, sometimes we hold on to these legends, if they can bring comfort to a bruised and bleeding heart. This legend has brought comfort to many bereaved people, simply by hearing it told. That being the case, I have no reservations about relating it as a means of alleviating their pain.

Rabbi Rifat Sonsino

As a congregational rabbi, I am often asked: "Rabbi, do we Jews believe in heaven and hell?" I surmise the real question behind this academic inquiry is: "What will happen to me after I die?"

The question is an old one, perhaps going back to the earliest stages of civilization. I am fascinated by many examples in world literature of humans attempting to break the cycle of death in order to attain immortality. I am also taken by the various descriptions of life in the world to come, which, I am certain, emerge from the creative imagination of those who project their wishes to an unknown realm. I am also familiar with those who claim to have journeyed to the otherworld and miraculously came back to tell it all.

As I get older, I become more aware of my mortality. At times, I find myself fantasizing about my afterlife. Given that I am the kind of person who asks for verifiable proof before accepting anything in life, I am drawn to the idea that I will live on through my deeds, my influence on others, and my children.

I remember vividly how excited I was after my doctoral dissertation on biblical law was published in 1980. This is my immortality, I said to myself. Even now, when one of my studies appears in print or an important project of mine gets off the ground successfully, I cheerfully smile within as I add another link to the chain of my modest contributions. I now realize, however, that my two children represent the better part of my legacy, even though when they were born I did not fully recognize the importance of their birth.

Death is an abyss, a mystery beyond our comprehension. I am amazed at the assertions of those who claim to know better. Am I afraid of what will happen? I don't even know what to be afraid of.

Intellectually I am more comfortable with the naturalistic notion that my "name" will remain alive as long as my family line continues and my work is appreciated by others. Yet, in the deepest recesses of my heart, I also wonder about what will happen to "me." I look at myself as representing an "energy." When I breathe my last, I am sure my body will disintegrate, but what will happen to the "energy" I have? Contrary to the medievalists, I do not hold that my "soul" is an entity. I am alive, I say, because my body is energized by an internal power that is hard to define. I find it hard to accept that this "spirit" will totally disappear. I prefer to embrace the statement "We are more than a memory slowly fading into the darkness. With our lives we give life. Something of us can never die" (*Gates of Prayer*, p. 627).

I am aware of my limitations and capabilities. I keep a deep trust in my ability to do what I do. Beyond that, I am left wondering what lies beyond the point of death. In the meantime, I am grateful for being alive, knowing full well that my limited existence makes each of my days more precious.

In Conclusion

The diversity of opinion about life after death within Judaism may be confusing for some, liberating for others. Obviously it would be comforting to "know" what to expect after we die. We could prepare ourselves for what is yet to come after we breathe our last. For better or for worse, however, this is not to be. We do not know. We cannot know.

Jewish philosophy, as you have seen, covers a spectrum of notions of the afterlife, ranging from Sheol, to existence in hell and paradise, to living on through the memories of others and with many shades of thinking in between. Yet we simply do not know. We only hope.

Facing this unknown, we need to turn toward life and its potential. In this sense, death can teach us a powerful lesson about life's value and how we must cherish it. Some time ago Rabbi Joshua Loth Liebman asserted that we must make up for the brevity of life by heightening its intensity. We must learn how to live life richly, creatively, and nobly.

This, we believe, would make our years on earth more precious and worthy of sanctity. It is with that same affirmation, therefore, that we conclude, as we echo the prayer of the Psalmist: "Teach us to number our days that we may obtain a heart of wisdom" (90:12).

ABOUT THE AUTHORS

Rifat Sonsino, a graduate of Hebrew Union College-Jewish Institute of Religion and presently the rabbi of Temple Beth Shalom in Needham, Massachusetts, holds a law degree from the University of Istanbul and a Ph.D. in Bible and Ancient Near Eastern Studies from the University of Pennsylvania.

Danial B. Syme, a rabbi and graduate of HUC-JIR, holds a doctorate in Education from Teachers College at Columbia University. For eleven years he has served as director of the Union of American Hebrew Congregations-Central Conference of American Rabbis Commission on Jewish Education and is now the vice president of the UAHC.

Rabbis Sonsino and Syme previously collaborated on *Finding God: Ten Jewish Responses*.